THE CONNOISSEUR'S GUIDE TO MEAT

THE CONNOISSEUR'S GUIDE TO MEAT

Jennie Milsom

Illustrated by Jane Laurie

STERLING

New York / London
www.sterlingpublishing.com

A Quintet book

STERLING and the distinctive Sterling logo are registered trademarks of Sterling Publishing
Co., Inc.

Library of Congress Cataloging-in-Publication Data Available

10 9 8 7 6 5 4 3 2 1

First Sterling edition published 2009.
Published by Sterling Publishing Co., Inc.
387 Park Avenue South, New York, NY 10016

This book was conceived, designed, and produced by
Quintet Publishing Limited
The Old Brewery, 6 Blundell Street
London N7 9BH, UK

Distributed in Canada by Sterling Publishing
c/o Canadian Manda Group, 165 Dufferin Street,
Toronto, Ontario, Canada M6K 3H6

Manufactured in China

ISBN 978-1-4027-7050-0

For information about custom editions, special sales, premium and
corporate purchases, please contact Sterling Special Sales
Department at 800-805-5489 or specialsales@sterlingpublishing.com.

Project Editor: Robert Davies
Designer: Emma Wicks
Copy Editor: Nicole Foster
Art Director: Michael Charles
Managing Editor: Donna Gregory
Publisher: James Tavendale

CONTENTS

What is meat?

Today, we often take for granted how easy and convenient it is to buy meat. For most of us it is hard to imagine having to trek farther than our local butcher or supermarket to choose from a wide selection of meat that has been carefully processed, preserved, and packaged. Yet everyday life for our ancestors was very different. Their diet, like ours, consisted of a mixture of meat and vegetables but the way they went about finding it was a much more hands-on experience. Animals and fish were hunted and killed with spears; berries, nuts, insects, and vegetables were foraged from bushes and trees. Venturing out into the wild with handmade tools to slaughter an animal and drag the bloody carcass home was as normal for our ancestors as jumping in a car and heading to the supermarket is for us.

Over the years, the word "meat" has come to mean the flesh of animals prepared for eating. It consists of water, protein, and fat and is made up of bundles of long, thin muscle fibers which become the recognizable grain of the meat. These fibers are surrounded by thin, glue-like sheets called connective tissue which fix the fibers to the bone, thereby allowing them to move with the animal. The harder the muscle fibers are worked, the more the connective tissue bulks up and the tougher the meat will be. Fat, which provides energy and insulation, is interspersed within the connective tissue and under the skin of the animal. Fat contributes to the tenderness of meat, too, by lubricating the muscle fibers, making them taste more succulent and juicy.

The human body is capable of breaking down most meat—our teeth can break the fibers apart and our intestines digest them—but the eating process is far more enjoyable if the meat has good flavor and texture.

Meat and farming

Humans have been farming animals for their meat for thousands of years. As breeds of cattle, pigs, and sheep have grown and diversified, so too has the choice of meat available to the consumer.

Methods of farming livestock can vary greatly. The way an animal is farmed for its meat depends on the individual farmer or organization, which in turn controls the environment the animals are exposed to. Farming has seen the introduction of chemicals in the form of pesticides and fertilizers that are used to control the land and optimize yields. Intensive livestock farming—where stock is high and animals are kept in close confines—often means the animals will require chemical-based medicines to prevent infection and disease. This type of farming may produce animals that become bored or aggressive, which can affect the quality of their meat.

Some farmers and organizations choose to farm organically. Organic farming is monitored by strict regulations to which farmers are bound to adhere in order to maintain their organic status. It uses natural substances and techniques for managing the land, such as introducing natural predators to control pests. Organic farming is viewed as being kinder to the environment and to human health, because

organic produce is free from the chemical residues that can be found in non-organic crops and meat.

Ultimately, the best-quality farmed meat comes from healthy animals that have been well reared from the day they were born until the moment they are slaughtered.

Slaughtering animals for their meat is usually carried out in a packing plant or harvesting facility. In the developed world, animal slaughter practice requires that animals be stunned before slaughter so that their suffering is lessened, because death occurs while the animal is unconscious. Once stunned, the neck arteries are severed and the excessive bleeding which ensues causes death by lack of oxygen to the brain. In the case of most halal and kosher slaughter practices, animals are not stunned before slaughter.

Besides cattle, pigs, and sheep, other animals slaughtered for their meat include horses, donkeys, and goats and kids. Horse meat is lean and densely textured and the carcass is cut up in much the same way as a cow's. Donkey meat is generally tough. It requires grinding down or slow cooking in moist heat and is typically used in stews and in sausage. Goat—known as kid when the animal is slaughtered young—has a similar flavor to lamb and beef. It is often stewed, made into curries, or barbecued.

Meat and health benefits

There are many positive reasons to include meat in your diet.
Lean meat is high in protein and contains all the essential
amino acids your body needs for energy, growth, and repair.

Lean beef, for example, contains high levels of iron, essential for the production of hemoglobin, which transports oxygen in the blood around the body. The iron content varies according to the different types and cuts but generally the redder the meat, the higher the iron content. Beef and lamb can contain up to three times as much iron as pork and a darker cut of pork from the shoulder will contain more iron than a paler piece from the loin.

Meat also contains zinc, which keeps the reproductive system healthy and plays a part in wound-healing. Vitamin B12 is present in meat—in particularly high amounts in beef and liver—and is essential for the development of red blood cells to prevent anemia and to protect the central nervous system.

However, eating meat should be part of a balanced diet. While its exact makeup varies according to the animal, its breed, and how it was reared, meat can be high in saturated fat and has sometimes been linked to high blood pressure, bowel cancer, and heart disease. If you are concerned about the fat content in meat, choose lean cuts and cook them on a roasting rack or ridged pan to allow excess fat to drain away.

The color of meat

Many factors, including the species of the animal, its diet, exercise, and age when slaughtered, as well as how the meat was processed and packaged, contribute to the color of meat. Color can be a reliable indicator of quality, yet brightly colored meat—while pleasing to the eye—does not necessarily guarantee freshness or flavor.

Beef

Beef should be deep red, not bright crimson. A brownish tinge or deeper brown color might suggest it has been aged. The longer meat is aged, the darker and more tender it will become. Fat should be creamy in color and visible bones should be pink. Flecks of fat—known as marbling—should run through the meat. Cuts of beef or lamb without marbling may lack flavor or moisture once cooked.

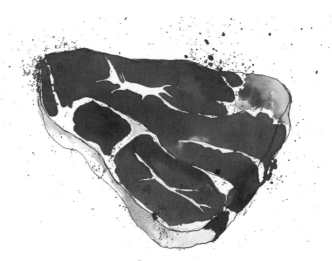

Lamb

Lamb should be pale pinkish-brown. It should not be bloody or gray. The younger the animal, the paler and more tender the meat will be. Meat from sheep that are older, or have enjoyed more exercise during their lifetime, will be darker in color. Fat around the edges should be creamy white, firm, and slightly crumbly with no yellow color at all. There should also be a fine marbling of fat through the meat, though less than you would find in a cut of beef. The bones in lamb cuts should be pink; a good example of this is lamb rib bones, named "cherry ribs" for their distinctive color. White bones indicate less tender meat from an older animal.

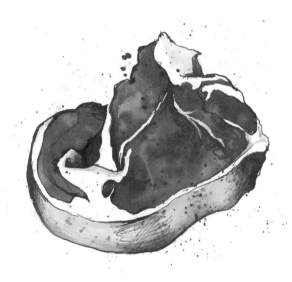

Pork

Pork should be pale pink and free from blood. Cuts that are too pale often become dry and stringy, and pork that is too dark will be tough though very juicy. Yellow or brown stains on the skin indicate poor-quality pork. Any small bones should be pinkish-blue in color. White, brittle bones indicate a much older animal with substantially tougher meat. The meat should be covered with a thin, even layer of dense, milk-white fat, and any skin should be thin and ideally without hair. Pork cuts may have marbled fat, but pork from a young animal (pale gray-pink) will be juicy and tender without the need for it.

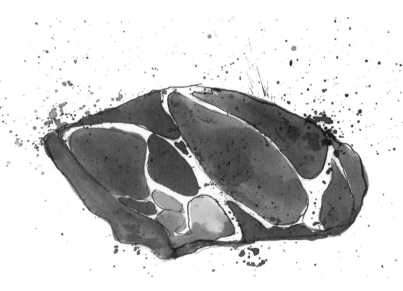

The texture of meat

The texture of meat can vary as much as its flavor. Tough steaks or chewy chops might taste great but they are rarely a pleasure to eat. So what makes some cuts more tender than others? First, some cuts of meat are naturally tougher than others—usually those taken from the parts of the animal that are nearer the ground and therefore work the hardest. These cuts contain more connective tissue and require slow cooking in moist heat or liquid to tenderize them.

The way the animal was reared and slaughtered, and its meat processed and stored, all contribute to the texture of the meat. The age of the animal is another factor that affects tenderness. Meat is made up of muscle fibers that increase in diameter as the animal ages. Therefore, a cut of meat from an older animal will be tougher and more fibrous than the same cut from a younger animal.

The way you prepare and cook meat will further influence its texture. A tough cut that is cooked quickly over a high heat will remain tough. Cook the same cut slowly in liquid over a low heat and the tough fibers and connective tissue will break down and tenderize. You can also improve the way you perceive the texture of meat by carving it across the grain, which reduces the length of the muscle fibers and makes the meat feel less chewy in the mouth.

When raw, all meat should feel firm and springy to the touch. The best cuts contain no gristle—a tough, inedible tissue—between the meat and the fat. Gristle is normally associated with older animals and can spoil the experience of chewing and the way the meat feels in the mouth.

Fat

Fat, which is described as being either saturated (solid at room temperature) or unsaturated (soft at room temperature), is one of the naturally occurring components of meat. We are often told that eating too much saturated animal fat is bad for us. However, when it comes to cooking, fat provides flavor and is essential for improving the texture of meat. Top fat—the layer under the skin that lies along the outside of a roast or steak— bastes the meat naturally by melting into it as it cooks. If you score through the top fat on a belly of pork or pork shoulder, you will be rewarded with succulent, flavorsome meat and the most pleasingly crisp crackling.

As well as a layer of top fat, red meat should also contain small flecks of the creamy white fat known as marbling. This fatty network breaks down during cooking, basting and tenderizing the meat as it does so, adding flavor and enhancing the eating quality. Meat that contains little or no marbling can taste tough, dry, and flavorless because the muscle fibers shrink and contract when cooked, squeezing out their moisture, rather than being basted in melting fat. For this reason, it is always advisable to choose red meat that has some of this marbling within the flesh, even if it also has an outside layer of top fat.

Lard is a white fat from pork used in slow-cooking and deep-frying, particularly in Europe and China. The term larding refers to a technique whereby strips of pork or beef fat are threaded into a lean roast using special needles. These fat strips behave in a similar way to natural marbling and melt into the meat as it cooks, tenderizing and flavoring it.

Other animal fats include suet, a hard, white beef fat taken from the kidneys that is used in pastries, dumplings, and puddings. Dripping, a common term in Great Britain, is the melted fat from a roast of meat, usually beef, which solidifies when cold. It can be reused in cooking or is traditionally spread on bread and sprinkled with salt and eaten cold.

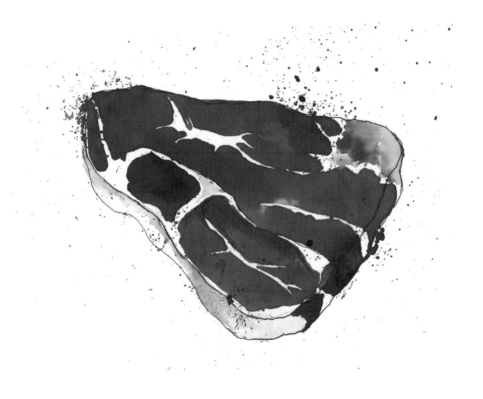

Processing a carcass

Once slaughtered, meat must undergo certain processing techniques before it is ready for sale and consumption. Immediately after slaughtering, the flesh is still warm and too soft to be eaten. Rigor mortis then sets in and the muscles contract and stiffen. Meat taken from a carcass during this time would be incredibly tough. When rigor mortis wears off, around 24 hours after slaughtering, the animal carcass can be hung to age or broken down into large cuts, known as primals.

Cutting up a carcass is a specialist skill and how it is carried out varies worldwide. The way a beef carcass is broken down in France, for example, is somewhat more intricate than the American or British method. These days, most carcasses are broken down into retail cuts and packaged at the processing plant, rather than being delivered whole to butchers.

Ultimately, the purpose of butchery is to produce recognizable cuts for the butcher or retailer and, in turn, for the professional or home cook. Good butchery should minimize waste, thereby making the consumption of meat economical to everyone involved and respectful to the animal.

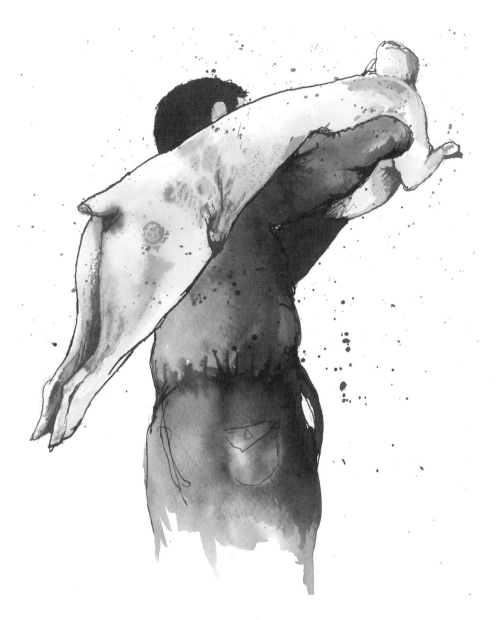

Aging meat

The taste and texture of meat—particularly that of beef and lamb—can be improved by aging. The aging process allows the fibers of the meat to break down and soften, enhancing the final flavor and the eating quality of the meat. Aging gives beef its characteristic gamey flavor and minimizes the metallic taste it can sometimes have. However, due to time and money constraints, not all meat is aged sufficiently, and some is not aged at all.

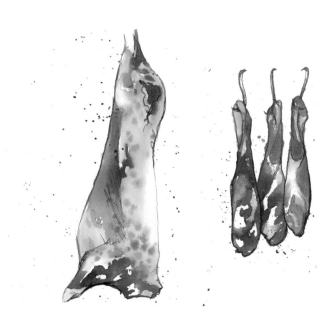

Aging is achieved by two methods: wet-aging and dry-aging. With wet-aging, cuts of meat are sealed in vacuum packs ready for retail, allowing them to mature in their own blood. This process is more incidental than by design, as the meat can age while in transportation and storage. Meat that is wet-aged loses no moisture and its final weight—and consequently its retail value—remains unchanged. Because of this, wet-aging is the cheaper and preferred option of many retailers, although some would argue that aging meat in its own blood while sealed in packs is neither effective nor desirable.

Meat can also be aged by hanging—a process often referred to by supermarkets as dry-aging. This is a slower process, taking up to four weeks, whereby the animal carcass, or cuts from it, is hung from hooks in a temperature-controlled environment. During hanging, the carcass undergoes a slow chemical change. As it dries out, the enzymes break down, tenderizing and concentrating the flavors of the flesh. The hanging or dry-aging process reduces the carcass's original weight by up to 20 percent, due to moisture loss. It is an expensive process, as the meat must be stored during hanging before it can be packed and distributed. Dry-aging does, however, produce more flavorful and tender meat than the wet-aging process. Whether meat is wet-aged or hung, its flavor and texture will be superior to meat that has been rushed through the processing chain and onto supermarket shelves without allowing it a chance to mature at all.

A good butcher

Where you choose to buy your meat can come down purely to convenience. You may head to your nearest supermarket or you might prefer to go out of your way to a meat specialist who offers what you consider to be the best product and service. Wherever you buy your meat, there are a few visual clues that can speak volumes about the quality of the meat a particular establishment has to offer.

First, the windows, walls, and floor of the store should be clean; if the visible public areas are dirty and unkempt, the state behind the scenes could well be worse. The meat should look fresh and appetizing. It should be displayed attractively and within its own type—for example beef, pork, and lamb should not be mixed together—and cuts should be labeled with detailed information. Meat should be shiny without being wet or slimy and should have a light, fresh scent; avoid anything with a strong odor.

An advantage of buying meat from a butcher is that less—or none—of the meat is likely to be prepacked. A good butcher will be happy to share his knowledge of meat and be able to advise you. As he has been involved in buying or processing the meat himself, he is likely to be able to answer any questions about it. You can ask him to order in a particular cut or prepare a cut in a certain way—for example, to bone a leg of lamb, to score the fat on a belly of pork, or to grind a piece of beef.

As well as asking for advice on which cuts to buy for a particular way of cooking or for a recipe, feel free to ask questions before you buy, including the following:

• whether the meat is organic or free-range

• how fresh the meat is—when the animal was slaughtered

• for how long the meat has been aged.

Packaging

Most meat on supermarket shelves is already pre-prepared and packaged. Packaging technology has come a long way since our grandparents', or even our parents', day. It is rare, though a delight, to find a traditional butcher, who still wraps meat loosely in brown, or "butcher's," paper.

Packaging is designed to be practical and, in the absence of a butcher on hand to answer queries, it should also provide sufficient information about its contents: the kind of meat and the cut it is, the use-by date, the price per pound, and the weight and price of the pack is the minimum information you should expect to see.

The traditional butcher might condemn the practice of vacuum-packing meat as being the worst kind of packaging there is, as the meat sits in a bloody marinade, sweating in its own juices and unable to "breathe." Breathing is important for meat because it allows the air to carry away excess moisture and the flavors to develop further. However, because vacuum-packing seals in the meat, it is considered to be one of the safest and most hygienic types of packaging. Vacuum-packed meat is convenient for retailers and consumers too, because it is easy to handle and transport.

If you buy vacuum-packed meat, remove it from the packaging, pat it dry with some paper towels.

Rewrap it in brown paper or transfer it to a plate and cover loosely with plastic wrap—bearing in mind that you will need to use it sooner than the specified date on the original packaging. If you are buying meat to use straight away, dry it off as soon as possible and allow it to breathe and come up to room temperature before cooking.

Another form of meat packaging is Modified Atmosphere Packaging (MAP). Meat is sealed in disposable containers with a mixture of gases, including oxygen, carbon dioxide, and nitrogen, which act as preservatives. Like vacuum-packing, this technique allows the meat to be transported easily and prolongs its shelf life.

Hygiene

If you prepare or cook meat, a basic knowledge of food hygiene is important for safeguarding your health. By following a few simple steps you can drastically reduce any risk of food poisoning. The most common cause of food poisoning is pathogenic bacteria which can thrive on raw food, and particularly on raw and cooked meat and meat products such as stews, gravies, and stocks.

Food poisoning is, at best, unpleasant, causing nausea, abdominal pain, vomiting, and diarrhea; for high-risk groups—the very young, the elderly, those with weakened immune systems, and pregnant women—food poisoning can be life-threatening.

• Meat should be kept chilled between 34 and 41°F (1 and 5°C). Bringing meat up to room temperature before cooking is fine provided it does not sit around for longer than necessary.

• Before preparing and handling meat, wash hands thoroughly and wash again between handling different types of meat. Always handle meat with utensils rather than hands.

• Raw and cooked meats should be prepared separately with clean knives and never on the same cutting board.

• Keep meat out of the "danger zone" temperature of 41–145°F (5–63°C), where bacteria multiply most rapidly. When heating or cooling food, particularly meat, do so as quickly as possible.

• Always check packaging for advice regarding storage and preparation. Don't be tempted to use meat which has passed its use-by date.

• Ensure your refrigerator is clean and that any spillages are wiped up with a sanitized cloth.

• Although beef can be eaten raw, it is advisable to cook at least the outside surface of a steak or roast in order to kill most bacteria. Beef that is cooked medium-rare will have an internal (core) temperature of 140–160°F (60–70°C).

• Lamb should be cooked until at least medium-rare—that is, until at least slightly pink and without blood—with a core temperature of 130–140°F (55–60°C).

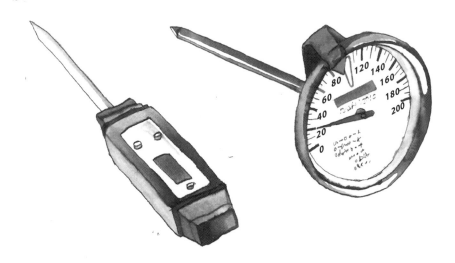

- Pork should be cooked until well done, with a minimum core temperature of 170°F (75°C).

- Cool, cover, and chill leftover meat as quickly as possible.

- Always reheat meat and meat dishes until piping hot with a core temperature of 160°F (70°C) for at least two minutes. Never reheat meat more than once.

- If you plan to eat anything that has come in contact with raw meat, such as a marinade, it must be heated to at least 170°F (75°C) before consumption. Never reuse marinades that have been in contact with meat.

Storing meat at home

- Put meat in the refrigerator as soon as you come home from shopping.

- Cooked meat should be cooled, then wrapped or covered before being chilled or frozen.

- Before chilling or freezing raw meat, rinse off any blood and pat it dry. Wrap in plastic film or put into a sealed container and refrigerate between 34 and 41°F (1 and 5°C) or freeze at 0°F (-18°C) or colder.

- Always thaw meat in the refrigerator, not at room temperature.

- Roasts (raw or cooked) will last in the refrigerator for three to five days. Smaller cuts, such as steaks and chops (raw or cooked), will last for two to four days (vacuum-packed meat will last longer—refer to packaging instructions).

- Never allow food to go moldy or rotten in the refrigerator.

Refrigerator know-how

When it comes to storing food, the key point to remember is to keep raw meat away from other food. All food, particularly raw and cooked meat, should be wrapped and placed in a dish or a sealed container before being chilled.

Top shelf
Vegetables and salad (salad crispers at the bottom of the refrigerator are commonly used but salad should ideally be stored above any raw meat)

In the door
Condiments and preserves (where the temperature fluctuates most)

Middle shelf
Cooked meat and meat products, such as cured meat

Bottom shelf
Raw meat

Very bottom shelf
Raw poultry
(the coldest spot)

Utensils for cooking meat

*It is better to have a few well-chosen, good-quality utensils than
a stack of cheaper ones that you are less likely to use. This list
provides an idea of useful equipment for all levels of cooking,
but there is no reason to rush out and buy everything at once—
you can add to your collection over time. The symbols below
indicate who is most likely to benefit from having each item.*

Butcher

Professional chef

Home cook

 Boning or meat-cutting table

Traditional work surface used by butchers to break a carcass
down into cuts

 Metal-mesh apron and gloves

For full protection against blades and other sharp objects

 Bone saw

For sawing through bones when breaking down a carcass

Cleaver

For chopping up large pieces of meat efficiently and quickly

Grinder

For breaking down pieces of meat into ground meat

Electric meat slicer

For slicing meat quickly, efficiently, and safely

Paring knife, cook's knife, boning knife

You are more likely to cut yourself with a blunt knife because of
the extra force required, so keep knives sharp

Sharpening steel or stone

Essential for keeping knives sharp

Wood, plastic, or nylon color-coded cutting boards

Whatever the type of board, always sanitize and wash
thoroughly with hot soapy water immediately after use

Additional useful equipment

- Spatula or palette knife

  For turning or lifting meat during cooking

- Carving board with spikes

  For holding meat in place during carving

- Carving knife and fork

  For steadying and carving meat as efficiently and safely as possible

- Poultry shears

  For trimming fat and cutting through small bones

- Meat thermometer

  For checking doneness of meat and core temperatures

- Meat tenderizer

  For batting out tougher pieces of meat before cooking

- Skewers

  To test for doneness and for holding pieces of meat in place

- Baster

  For distributing fat and juices over meat as it cooks

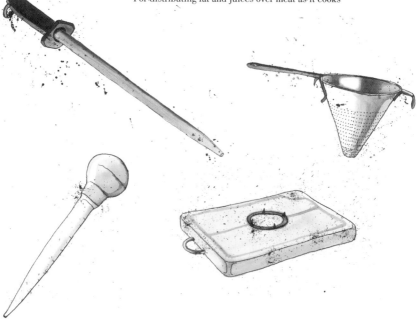

- Pastry brush

  For brushing over oil and marinades
- String or silicon bands

  For tying up cuts of meat before roasting
- Long-handled tweezers

  For removing small, awkward bones
- Conical gravy strainer

  For removing lumps in gravy before serving
- Casserole dish

  For roasting pieces of meat
- Dutch oven

  For cooking pot-roasts, braises, and stews
- Selection of sturdy deep and shallow roasting pans

  Choose pans that can be used on the stovetop as well as
  in the oven
- Heavy skillet

  Ideally cast-iron or one that can be used on the stovetop as well as
  in the oven
- Selection of heavy saucepans with lids

  For stocks, sauces, and accompaniments; heavy bases provide even
  heat distribution

Tenderizing meat

***Some cuts of meat are naturally more tender than others.
Tougher cuts require tenderizing before they can be enjoyed.***

This can be done in a number of ways:

• By slow cooking in moist heat or liquid, either by poaching, pot-roasting, stewing, or braising. This breaks down muscle fibers and connective tissue.

• By pounding. Pounding with a meat tenderizer or rolling pin changes the composition of the muscle fibers, making the meat more tender. For ease, cover the meat in a layer of plastic wrap or nonstick parchment paper before bashing it flat.

• By grinding. Grinding breaks down the connective tissue and any tough fibers in the meat, making it feel more tender in the mouth.

• By marinating. A marinade is a flavored liquid that usually contains an acid, such as wine, lemon juice, or vinegar, combined with aromatic and fragrant flavors, such as fresh or dried herbs, crushed or whole spices, garlic, ginger, or sugar. Submerging meat in an acid-based marinade before cooking adds flavor and softens the muscle fibers. A marinade should be a balance of flavors that enhance and complement, rather than overpower, the flavor of the meat.

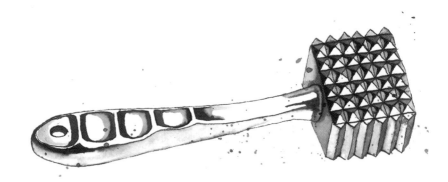

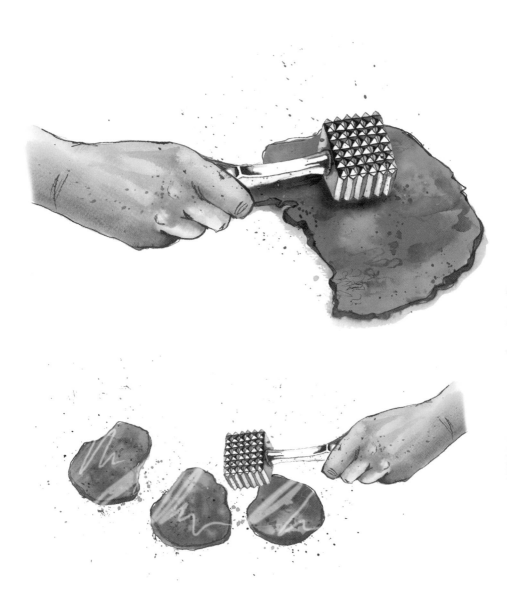

Marinades

A marinade may be cooked before it is applied to the meat. Cooking a marinade—for example, dissolving sugar in the liquid—allows its ingredients to meld together and become syrupy, helping it to coat the meat. A cooked marinade must be cooled before adding the meat.

Use nonmetallic dishes when marinating because metals can react with the acid in the marinade. Turn the meat regularly to coat it evenly in the marinade. Alternatively, use a resealable plastic food-safe bag, which will allow the marinade to penetrate fully into the meat.

The length of time the meat is left in the marinade will depend on its size and cut. The longer the meat marinates, the softer its fibers will become and the more it will take on the flavors of the marinade. Smaller pieces of meat will soak up the marinade more quickly than larger cuts. Tough stewing cuts, such as chuck, can be marinated in the refrigerator for up to three days. A naturally tender cut of meat—such as beef tenderloin—requires only brief marinating to enhance the flavor.

The marinade liquid may also be added to the pan with the meat, provided it is brought up to a boil before serving. If the marinade is not required in the dish, the meat should be lifted from it and patted dry before cooking.

Preparing meat for roasting

To prepare a boneless or bone-in roast

Preheat the oven. Put the meat on a board and pat it dry with paper towel. Using a sharp knife or scissors, trim away any excess fat.

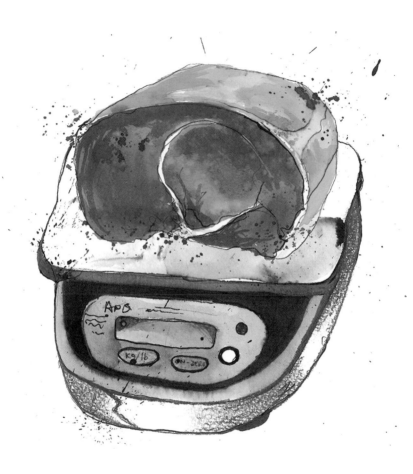

Weigh the meat and calculate the cooking time. Allow around 6 ounces meat per person for a boneless roast; 8 ounces for a bone-in roast.

Heat a roasting pan over a medium heat. Season the roast with salt and pepper and carefully add to the pan, fat-side down. If the cut of meat is lean or contains no top fat, you may need to add a little oil to the pan first. Quickly sear or brown the roast all over, turning with spoons or tongs. Remove from the pan.

Put a rack into the roasting pan and sit the browned roast on top. Transfer to a preheated oven to roast (see Roasting, page 45). Roasting fattier meats, such as pork and lamb, on a rack set within the roasting pan allows excess fat to drain away.

You may wish to skip the searing step and roast the meat at a higher temperature for the first 20 minutes (see cooking times on page 45).

To stuff and tie a boneless roast

A boned roast of beef, pork, or lamb can be opened out, stuffed, and rolled before roasting to add extra texture and flavor.

Place the roast on a board and trim away any excess fat with a sharp knife or scissors. Lay the roast fat-side down on the board and open it out flat (cut the meat open with a knife if necessary).

Spoon over the stuffing in an even layer.

Roll up the meat to enclose the stuffing, so the fat is on the outside. Tie with string at evenly spaced intervals.

Slash the layer of top fat with a sharp knife, then season with salt and pepper.

Put the meat on a rack in a roasting pan and transfer it to a preheated oven to roast.

Cooking techniques

We cook meat to make it safe to eat and easier to digest, and to improve its flavor and texture. Applying heat alters its texture and color. As red meat cooks, it changes from a deep red color to a paler pink and through to a gray-brown. Its fibers contract and the water and juices within are squeezed out.

Before cooking meat, remove it from the refrigerator to let it come up to room temperature. This will help it cook evenly and ensure that the calculated cooking times will be accurate.

Roasting

Roasting is a method of cooking in the oven that requires high heat and a little fat. Basting meat—coating it with hot fat from the pan—is necessary if the meat is lean, though if the meat has a top layer of fat and good marbling the fat will melt into the meat as it cooks and basting will not be essential.

Roasting is best suited to tender cuts of meat that will cook relatively quickly and are not dried out by high heat. Slow roasting at a lower temperature can make some cuts of meat more succulent and tender. Tougher cuts, which contain more connective tissue, will require roasting for longer at a lower temperature.

The table below is a guide to the fastest way of roasting boneless cuts without compromising the meat's succulence. Weight for weight, a boneless roast will take longer to cook than a bone-in roast, as bones conduct heat and speed up the cooking time.

MEAT	CUTS AVAILABLE FOR ROASTING	METHOD
Beef	Sirloin, tenderloin, and rib	*Preheat the oven to 425°F (220°C). Brown the meat for 20 minutes, then reduce the temperature to 325°F (160°C) and roast for an additional 15 minutes per pound for rare, 20 minutes per pound for medium and 30 minutes per pound for well done.*
Pork	Loin, leg, and shoulder	*Pork is usually cooked until the meat is well done. Preheat the oven to 425°F (220°C). Brown the meat for 20 minutes, then reduce the temperature to 375°F (190°C) and roast for an additional 25 minutes per pound, plus 25 minutes at the end of the calculated time.*
Lamb	Loin, leg, and shoulder	*Lamb is traditionally cooked until pink or rosy inside. Preheat the oven to 425°F (220°C). Brown the meat for 20 minutes, then reduce the temperature to 375°F (190°C) and continue roasting for 20 minutes per pound for pink. For well-done lamb, roast for an additional 20 minutes at the end of the calculated time.*

Frying

Frying is a fast method of cooking in a skillet. It is ideal for small, tender cuts of meat, such as chops, cutlets, and steaks.

Use a wide, uncovered pan. Oil the pan and preheat it until it is hot and the oil is rippling before adding the meat. Do not allow the oil to smoke in the pan because it will scorch the meat when it is added.

Pat the meat dry with paper towel before adding it to the pan, otherwise it will not brown and caramelize sufficiently.

Fry the meat in batches if the pan is not big enough. Overcrowding the pan will lower the cooking temperature and result in the meat becoming tough and dry.

The cooking time with frying depends more on the thickness of the meat than on its weight.

Char-grilling

This is a method of cooking meat quickly over a high heat in a shallow, ridged, cast-iron pan or skillet to achieve either blackened diagonal lines or a criss-cross effect on both sides of the meat. It is a relatively healthy way of cooking meat, as it requires minimal cooking oil and any excess fat from the meat can drain away. Before adding the meat, the pan is heated over a high heat and brushed with oil to keep the meat from sticking. During cooking, the meat can be brushed with a marinade or extra oil if it is looking dry.

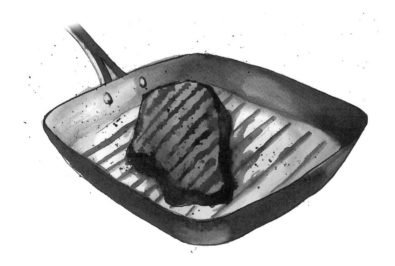

Stir-frying

Stir-frying is a fast way of cooking strips, cubes, or slices of meat in a round or flat-bottomed wok or large skillet. The oil is heated in the pan until hot and rippling and the meat—often marinated for extra flavor—is then added and cooked quickly over a high heat, while being moved around constantly with a spatula.

Once seared, the meat can be removed from the pan. Chopped vegetables, a marinade, and any other ingredients can then be added and cooked quickly before the meat is returned to the pan to heat through and mingle with the flavors.

Because stir-frying is such a fast method of cooking, having all the ingredients ready-prepared and close at hand before you start cooking is vital—there will be little time for chopping once cooking begins.

Broiling

Broiling is a method of cooking whereby direct heat is applied from above.

Just as preheating the oven is essential before roasting meat, it is important to preheat the broiler to its highest setting before adding the meat. A strong heat will help to give the meat a lovely caramelized flavor.

Ideally, broiled meat should be slightly charred and crisp on the outside and succulent and juicy within. Only fairly thin, tender cuts are suitable for broiling and they should be brushed with a little oil or melted butter first.

Browning and searing

Browning meat in hot oil at a high temperature before cooking it more slowly enhances its flavor and appearance. Browning is often necessary for cubes, slices, and strips of meat destined for stews, pot-roasts, and braises. Searing usually refers to browning a roast. Browning or searing in a hot pan on the stovetop or at a high temperature in the oven will caramelize the outside of the meat and seal in its juices. Sometimes a recipe will require dusting the meat in flour before browning; the addition of this starch will thicken any liquid added to the pan later, turning it into a rich sauce.

Braising

For a braise, the meat is first browned with a combination of finely diced vegetables such as carrots, celery, and onion, known as a "mirepoix," in a casserole or Dutch oven on the stovetop or in the oven. Stock or other flavorsome liquid is then added and the dish is covered with a tight-fitting lid. Braises are made with meat which is reasonably lean and rich in connective tissue. During cooking the vegetables break down slightly and, along with the natural gelatins released from the meat, they thicken the liquid, resulting in a deliciously sticky sauce. As liquid is required, braising is more like a stew than a pot-roast. Using a good-quality stock will give the braise an intense depth of flavor.

Poaching

Simmering meat gently in boiling liquid on the stovetop or in the oven is known as poaching. It is suitable for cooking both tender and tougher cuts. The liquid should not be allowed to come to a vigorous boil because this will cause the meat to disintegrate. Take care not to overcook the meat, because it will dry out and become fibrous. It is common to flavor the cooking water with vegetables and herbs, such as chopped onions, carrots, bay leaves, and a bouquet garni, or herb bundle; this flavored liquid can then be served as a broth or as part of the finished dish.

Pot-roasting

Pot-roasting is similar to braising, except that it does not require stock or liquid other than the cooking fat, although in some instances a little additional liquid is used. It is therefore a drier method of cooking than braising, relying on the meat's own juices to provide moisture. The term "roasting" is confusing, because the meat is not so much roasted as baked in a casserole dish or Dutch oven with a tight-fitting lid on the stovetop or in the oven. Meat used for pot-roasting is usually fattier than that for braising and the result should taste roasted. The meat is first browned, then cooked on a mirepoix of diced vegetables with the cooking fat and sometimes a little stock or liquid. The meat should fit snugly into the dish; if the dish is too roomy, the meat is likely to dry out. Pot-roasting is a great way of tenderizing tougher cuts. The diced vegetables can be served with the meat or broken down and used in an accompanying sauce.

Stewing

For a stew, meat is cut into cubes and browned before being simmered on the stovetop or in the oven in plenty of liquid, such as stock, water, beer, or wine. The cooking liquid forms part of the finished dish and, toward the end of cooking, can be thickened with flour, cornstarch, or a paste of butter and flour (beurre manié) to form a gravy-like sauce. Chopped onions, mushrooms, and carrots can be added with the meat to provide extra color, texture, and flavor. This moist, slow cooking method is ideal for tenderizing tougher cuts of meat; cuts with a generous amount of connective tissue and marbling make for the best stews. Take care not to overcook the stew, because the meat will disintegrate or become stringy. White stews are made without browning the meat first; as a result, the finished stew is paler in color.

Spit-roasting

A whole animal carcass—usually a pig or a sheep—may be spit-roasted over an open fire. This is a great way of feeding a crowd and is something of a celebratory meal. The carcass is mounted and tied with wire onto the spit, then rubbed or brushed with oil. With pork, the skin is first scored all over and rubbed with salt (this will produce the most delicious crackling). The spit and carcass are then suspended above burning embers and turned at intervals to allow the meat to become an even golden brown. After this initial browning, the spit is moved farther from the heat to let the meat cook slowly and evenly while the spit turns. The natural flavors of the meat are sealed inside and are enhanced by the aroma of the burning embers. To ensure that the meat roasts evenly, it is necessary to allow time for the carcass to come up to room temperature before being spit-roasted—this can take 12 hours or longer, depending on its size.

Stocks

Stocks are clear, deeply flavored liquids used for stews, soups, gravies, braises, and sauces. They are quick to prepare, and just require some time to bubble away. A brown stock is made from beef, lamb, or pork bones. It is richly flavored and deeply colored because the raw meat bones are first roasted until they are golden and caramelized. Any meat clinging to the bones will add extra flavor to the stock.

The roasted bones are then fully immersed in a deep-sided pan of cold water with a selection of chopped vegetables, such as leek, carrot, onion, celery, and herbs, such as parsley stalks, thyme, and bay leaves. The liquid is brought up to a boil and simmered for several hours until it takes on the rich flavor of the bones and other ingredients and has sufficiently reduced in volume; stocks are thickened by reduction, not by adding flour. As the stock simmers, any fat rising to the surface should be skimmed off with a spoon. Use stocks in the same meat dishes as the bones from which they have been made. A good stock will taste flavorful enough to be enjoyed on its own as a broth.

Gravy

Gravy is a popular accompaniment to roasted meats. It is traditionally made from the pan juices given out by the meat as it cooks. After cooking, the roast or pieces of meat are lifted from the pan and kept warm while the gravy is prepared. Excess fat is removed from the pan, leaving any brown juices and caramelized bits from the meat; these add plenty of flavor.

The pan is returned to the stovetop and a small quantity of liquid, such as wine or water, is stirred into the flavorsome juices (this is known as "deglazing"). Stock is gradually stirred in—the type of stock should match the meat that the gravy will be served with—the liquid is brought to a simmer and allowed to reduce until slightly thickened. Some gravies are thickened by stirring a little flour into the meat juices and letting it cook for a few minutes before the stock is added. The flavor of gravy can be enhanced by additional ingredients, such as redcurrant jelly and fresh herbs.

Carving

Carving is the process of slicing roasted meat into portions before serving. The cooked roast is removed from the pan, covered loosely with foil, and left in a warm place for up to half an hour. This is known as resting, and it allows the juices to redistribute throughout the meat, ensuring it is succulent before carving.

The meat should then be transferred to a carving board, ideally one with spikes to hold the underside of the joint in place. Use a carving fork in one hand to steady the roast, and slice pieces of meat from the joint with a sharp carving knife. Boneless roasts are easier to carve than those containing a bone or several bones, which require a certain amount of skill to cut around in order to release the meat.

Accompaniments

Various sauces and accompaniments have become popular to serve with meat. Many accompaniments are now sold readymade in jars and packets but it is easy—and often more rewarding in terms of flavor and cost—to make your own. Whether you buy or make your accompaniments, their purpose should be the same: to enhance and complement the flavor of the meat with which they are served.

Some traditional accompaniments

- **Horseradish sauce for roast beef**
  For the best, most pungent flavor, use freshly grated horseradish mixed with a generous amount of lightly whipped cream or crème fraîche. Season with salt and pepper and a little sugar to taste.

- **Applesauce for roast pork**
  Cook peeled, sliced apples in a pan with a splash of water and a squeeze of lemon juice until softened and breaking up. Beat in a little sugar and butter until the sauce is thick and smooth. Best served warm.

- **Mint sauce for roast lamb**
  Put some freshly chopped mint leaves into a heatproof bowl. Cover with boiling water and equal quantities of sugar and white wine vinegar. Mix well to dissolve the sugar, adding a little more of either sugar or vinegar to balance the flavors. Season and serve cold.

Preserving, curing, and cold-smoking

Before commercial refrigeration, preserving was the only way of ensuring that meat and fish were free from decay and safe to eat. Cured meats provided essential nutrients for sailors at sea for months on end. Traditional curing uses salt to draw water from the meat, thereby reducing its volume, concentrating its flavor, and lengthening its lifespan. Herbs, spices, and sugar can be mixed with the salt for extra flavor. Today, a lot of commercially preserved meat has been cured using chemicals and flavorings, and the ancient technique of preserving or curing food at home has almost disappeared. Curing meat by injecting liquid—rather than extracting it—to bulk up its weight is not uncommon.

Traditional curing requires few ingredients—a good-quality piece of meat, salt, air, and time. To cure meat at home, choose a wooden, plastic, or ceramic container (avoid metal as it can react with the salt) and rub the meat—such as pork belly, pork leg, or beef brisket—with handfuls of salt. Cover loosely, then store in a cool place, changing the salt every day for a week.

Wet-curing with brine is another way of preserving meat. A basic brine mix is three parts water to one part salt, to which herbs and spices can be added for flavor. Wine, beer, or fruit juice can be used as part of the liquid. The meat is submerged in the liquid, allowing it to release its water gradually, thereby taking on the flavors of the brine.

After meat has been wet- or dry-cured, it is rinsed and can then be air-dried. This process can take up to several months and it allows the flavors of the meat to develop even further. Air-drying is a common practice for cured pork and beef, such as salami, Parma ham, bresaola, and African biltong.

Cured beef, lamb, and pork can also be cold-smoked. This is a slower process than hot-smoking and further preserves and intensifies the flavor of cured meat.

Cold-smoking requires low heat (150°F/65°C or lower) and can be achieved in a smoking box, which resembles a small, covered oven filled with a layer of woodchips and containing a rack for the meat to sit on. Cold-smoking can also be achieved by hanging cured meat over a smoldering log fire. Smoked meats include beef jerky and bacon.

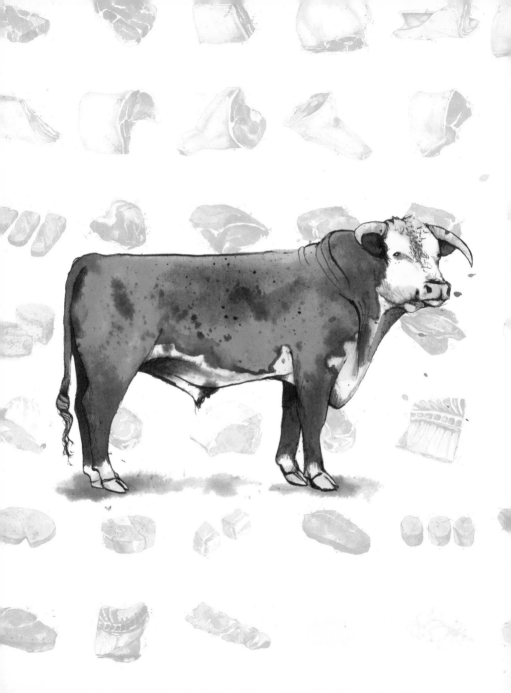

BEEF

Beef—the name of the meat taken from a bovine animal or carcass—is hugely popular all over the world. The carcass is broken down into cuts, known as primals, which can be categorized into three larger groups: middle meats, end meats, and thin meats. Almost all parts of the animal are eaten. Beef is cooked and prepared in all sorts of ways, from simple grilling or frying to roasting and stewing; it can also be served raw, as in steak tartare or carpaccio.

Primal cuts

The primal cuts are those made in the initial stage of butchering. They may be sold whole, or subdivided into smaller cuts for sale to home cooks.

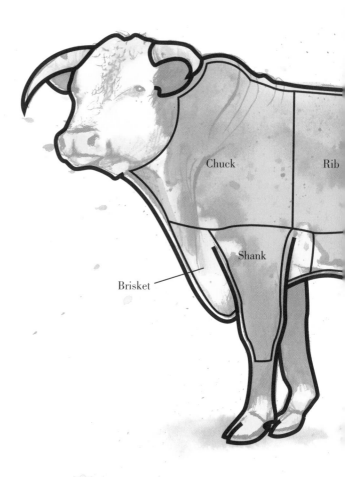

Chuck

Rib

Shank

Brisket

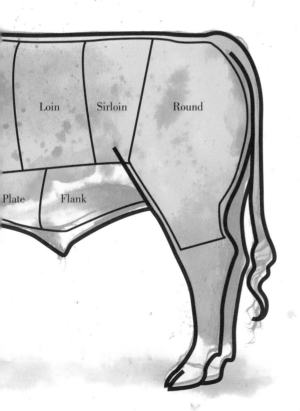

Chuck

The chuck is the largest of the eight primal cuts from the beef animal or carcass. It consists of the large section of shoulder and includes the first five ribs.

The chuck breaks down into two sub-primals: the chuck roll and the boneless shoulder clod in the lower portion. A sub-cut referred to as shoulder comes from the shoulder clod; most other sub-cuts come from the chuck roll. The blade is in the upper part of the chuck. Chuck can be divided into bone-in and boneless cuts for roasts and steaks and is often ground and used in hamburgers, and particularly in Salisbury steaks, which are seasoned with chopped onion, shaped into a steak, fried or grilled, and served with gravy and onions.

Flavor

This primal provides numerous economical cuts which are extremely flavorful. They contain plenty of connective tissue, which breaks down during cooking.

Cooking

To break down the connective tissue and tenderize the meat, chuck cuts demand long, slow cooking in liquid, such as pot-roasting and stewing.

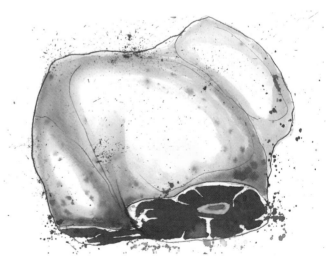

Chuck-eye roast and steaks

The chuck-eye roast is a boneless cut from the center of the chuck roll. It can be cut into steaks.

Flavor

This is a particularly tender cut of chuck with good flavor.

Cooking

The roast is best suited to braising or roasting until medium-rare. Steaks can be grilled, broiled, or fried.

Also known as

Boneless chuck roll, Scotch tender, boneless chuck fillet, mock tender steak, boneless chuck steak, chuck tender steak, and chingolo *(Spanish).*

Substitutes

Top blade roast, top blade steak.

Chuck pot-roast

This is a cut from the arm, shoulder, or blade chuck and can be bone-in or boneless. Cuts from the chuck pot-roast are known as arm steaks and arm Swiss steaks.

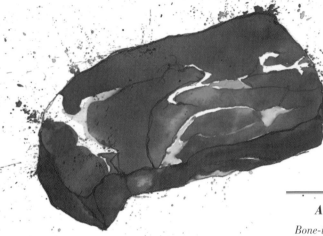

Flavor

Chuck pot-roast has great flavor. It is usually well marbled and contains plenty of connective tissue.

Cooking

Chuck pot-roast requires long, slow cooking and is best suited to stewing, braising, or pot-roasting.

Also known as

Bone-in roasts include arm pot-roast, blade roast, cross-rib pot-roast (also known as English roast), shoulder roast, and épaule (French). Boneless roasts include bolar roast, chuck-eye roast, arm roast, boneless cross rib, center-cut chuck roast, Diamond Jim roast, top blade (flatiron roast), shoulder clod roast, chuck roll, and chuck wagon roast. Blade roast includes the top blade steak (flatiron steak) and the under blade roast.

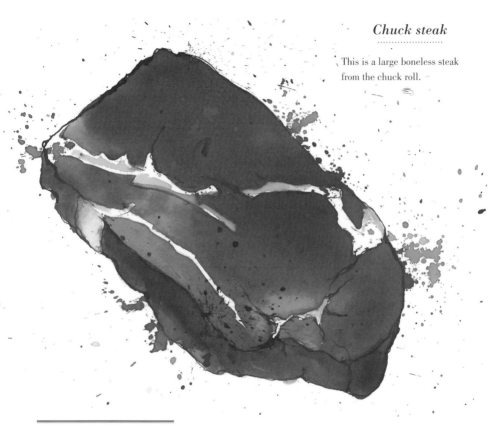

Chuck steak

This is a large boneless steak from the chuck roll.

Flavor

Chuck steak is a relatively tough and chewy cut but it has good flavor.

Substitute

Round steak.

Cooking

It requires tenderizing by slow, moist cooking and is best marinated before being slowly braised.

Denver cut

This is a relatively new steak cut from the chuck roll. It offers great value and is fast gaining in popularity.

Flavor

Thanks to its superb marbling, Denver cut is incredibly tender and juicy.

Cooking

It can be marinated or seasoned with a rub before being broiled, grilled, or fried.

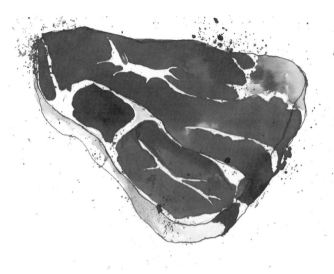

7-bone pot-roast

This economical cut from the shoulder clod takes its name from the shoulder blade bone contained within it, which is shaped like the number seven. It can be cut into steaks called 7-bone steaks.

Flavor

The 7-bone pot-roast requires long, slow cooking in liquid, such as stewing, braising, or pot-roasting, to tenderize it.

Also known as

Center cut pot-roast, chuck 7-bone roast, chuck roast center cut, and 7-bone roast. 7-bone steaks are also known as Texas broil.

Substitute

Arm roast.

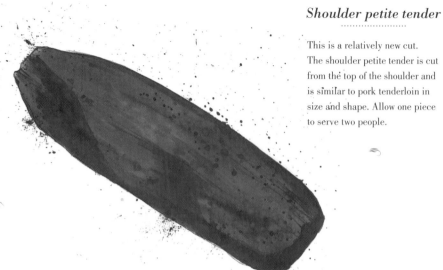

Shoulder petite tender

This is a relatively new cut. The shoulder petite tender is cut from the top of the shoulder and is similar to pork tenderloin in size and shape. Allow one piece to serve two people.

Flavor

The shoulder petite tender is sold ready trimmed, so it is lean yet naturally juicy.

Cooking

It can be roasted, grilled, or cut into medallions and fried.

Also known as

Petite filet, shoulder tender roast, and shoulder tender medallions

Shoulder pot-roast and shoulder steaks

This is a boneless, economical cut from the shoulder clod. Shoulder
steaks are cut from the shoulder pot-roast.

Flavor

*The shoulder pot-roast can
be incredibly flavorsome,
if somewhat tough.*

Cooking

*It becomes meltingly tender
with long, slow cooking and
benefits from marinating
before being braised.*

Also known as

Shoulder roast.

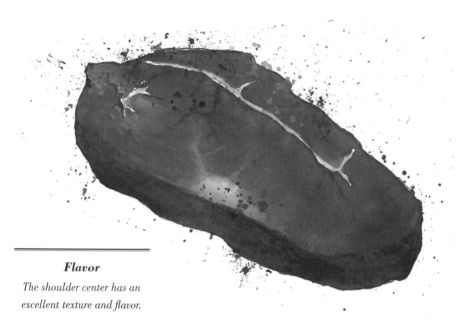

Flavor

The shoulder center has an excellent texture and flavor.

Cooking

It can be grilled or broiled and often benefits from being marinated or braised.

Also known as

Clod heart and mock brisket. Steaks are known as beef filet and ranch-style steak, barbecue steak, cross-rib steak, full steak, and shoulder clod steak.

Substitute

Sirloin.

Shoulder center

Shoulder center is a cheaper alternative to sirloin. It can be roasted whole or cut into steaks. Leftovers are great sliced cold in salads and sandwiches the next day.

Chuck boneless short ribs

Chuck boneless short ribs are almost square in shape. As they are cooked in liquid they are best eaten with a knife and fork rather than with fingers. They are known as flanken-style short ribs when they consist of just the first five ribs and are cut across the bone, and English-style short ribs when they are cut parallel to the bone.

Flavor
Boneless short ribs contain some fat and connective tissue.

Cooking
In order to become lovely and tender they require slow, moist cooking, such as braising.

Also known as
Chuck short ribs, boneless short ribs, and boneless country-style beef chuck ribs.

Brisket

Brisket is one of the thin meats and is taken from the lower chest of the beef animal or carcass beneath the first five ribs. Brisket is an inexpensive boneless cut, weighing around 16 pounds, and is used to make commercial corned beef.

Flavor

Brisket can be incredibly flavorsome and tender if cooked slowly. For best results, choose well-marbled brisket.

Cooking

Brisket must be cooked slowly in moist heat, such as in a braise or pot-roast. It responds well to marinating and smoking (it is particularly popular for smoking on the barbecue). It is worth trimming off some fat before cooking but brisket will dry out and toughen if it is too lean.

Substitute

Bottom round roast.

Brisket flat cut

This is a large, lean, flat cut weighing up to 9 pounds.

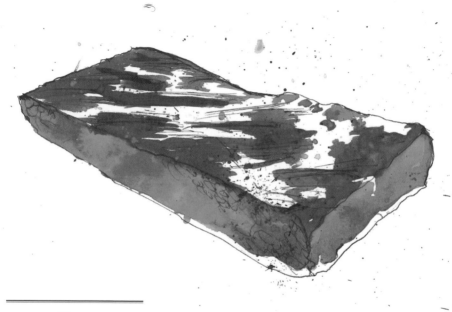

Flavor

Brisket flat cut has great flavor and texture.

Cooking

It requires slow, moist cooking over a low heat and is therefore suitable for pot-roasting and braising.

Also known as

Deckle off, first cut, flat half, navel end brisket, thin cut, pecho (Spanish), and poitrine (French).

Brisket point cut

This is a smaller, fattier cut of brisket. It is triangular in shape.

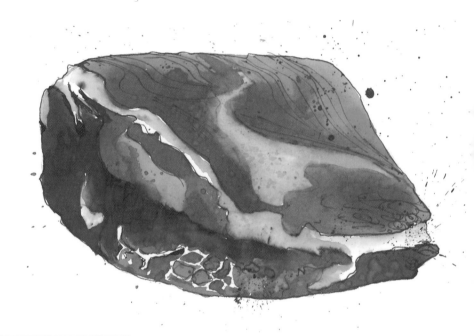

Flavor

*Brisket point cut has more
flavor than brisket flat cut.*

Cooking

*Brisket point cut is best suited
to pot-roasting.*

Also known as

Point cut and deckle.

Rib

The rib primal weighs around 35 pounds and is taken from the animal's back between the chuck and the loin. The rib is one of the middle cuts of the beef animal or carcass and consists of ribs 6 to 12 and part of the backbone.

It also contains the rib-eye muscle, which runs through its center. This muscle is barely exercised and is therefore incredibly tender. The rib is one of the most sought-after of all the primals and is therefore an expensive choice.

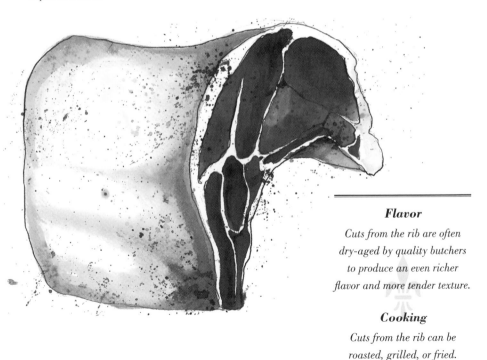

Flavor

Cuts from the rib are often dry-aged by quality butchers to produce an even richer flavor and more tender texture.

Cooking

Cuts from the rib can be roasted, grilled, or fried.

Rib roast and rib steaks

The rib roast is considered to be one of the best cuts of beef and includes between two and seven ribs. It is juicy, tender, and well marbled and is an impressive roast to serve at the table. The term "prime rib" refers to a rib roast in general and is not necessarily an indication of the quality. Rib steaks and chops are cut from the rib roast. If the meat is cut away to expose the bone, it is known as a Frenched rib chop.

Flavor

The rib roast contains plenty of fat marbling which breaks down and melts as it cooks, giving it an incredible texture and rich flavor.

Cooking

It is tender enough to be cooked by dry heat, such as roasting. A standing rib roast is roasted in a standing position with the ribs stacked vertically.

Also known as

Bone-in rib-eye roast, fore rib (British), prime rib, rib-eye, and rib-roast. Rib steaks are also known as beauty steak, cowboy steak, market steak, shell steak, Spencer steak, and entrecôte (French).

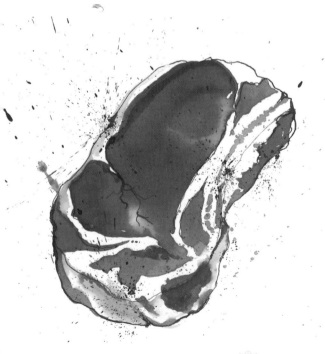

Rib-eye roast and rib-eye steak

The rib-eye roast is a boneless cut that can be cut into rib-eye steaks. Both roast and steaks contain part of the tender rib-eye muscle.

Flavor

Rib-eye roast and steaks are well marbled, extremely succulent, tender, and full of flavor.

Cooking

The rib-eye roast is best suited to roasting and braising.

Substitute

Tenderloin roast or rib roast.

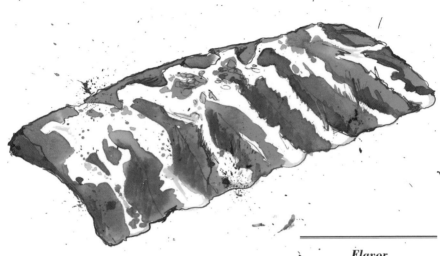

Back ribs

Back ribs are the bones that are removed from a rib roast to make it a rib-eye roast. They are usually sold in slabs. If they are boned they are called boneless short ribs. The Royal Rib is the sixth rib on its own, partially cut from the bone, then rolled and tied.

Flavor

Back ribs are slightly fatty without a great deal of meat, but tasty nonetheless.

Cooking

They are often marinated before cooking. They are best grilled, broiled, or barbecued.

Also known as

Rib caps, rib bones, Texas ribs, and rib lifters.

Substitute

Short ribs.

Hanging tender

The hanging tender is an interior cut which hangs from the last rib below the tenderloin. It is not technically classed under any primal; rather, it is its own individual cut. The hanging tender is often ground and used in burgers and is a popular cut in France.

Flavor

The hanging tender is packed with flavor.

Cooking

It should be cooked quickly over a high heat. It is often marinated before cooking to tenderize it.

Also known as

Hanging steak, hanger steak, bistro steak, boxeater steak, body skirt, onglet (French), and solomillo de pulmon (Spanish).

Substitute

Skirt steak or flank steak.

Plate and flank

*The plate and flank are taken from the belly section
of the beef carcass and are part of the thin meats.*

The plate weighs around 30 pounds and is a continuation of the brisket primal. It continues to the flank,
toward the rear underside of the animal. The flank weighs around 20 pounds. It is boneless and can be cut into
steaks. The short plate is part of the upper part of the plate primal and is where the short ribs are taken from.

Flavor

*The plate and flank can be
relatively tough and are not
generally considered to be a
good cut for roasts.*

Cooking

*Flank is often used for
ground beef or cut into
strips for fajitas.*

Skirt steak

Taken from the short plate, the skirt steak is long and thin. There is one on each side of the carcass and it can be divided into either the inside or the outside. The inside skirt is more desirable as it contains less of the membrane from the diaphragm.

Flavor

Skirt steak is well marbled and is particularly flavorful.

Cooking

Because of its loose texture and rich flavor, skirt steak responds well to marinating for up to 24 hours. It can then be broiled or fried, though care must be taken not to overcook it, which will toughen the meat. Strips of skirt steak are often used in Mexican fajitas.

Also known as

Rump skirt, thin steak (British), and Philadelphia steak.

Flank steak

This is a small, moderately priced boneless steak weighing up to 2 pounds. Strips of flank steak are often used in Mexican fajitas and in Asian cuisine. It is one of the cuts often used in London Broil.

Flavor

Flank steak is tougher than the loin or rib steaks but flavorsome nonetheless. To improve its tenderness it is often cut across the grain.

Cooking

It is best suited to being marinated, then broiled or fried until rare or medium-rare.

Also known as

Jiffy steak, bavetta (Italian), and bavette (French).

Substitute

Hanging tender or skirt steak.

Short ribs

Short ribs can be taken from any of the sections of 12 ribs including
those in the short plate. Ribs taken from here can be expensive but are
more economical than chuck ribs.

Cooking

*Short ribs can be braised,
slow-roasted, or boiled. They
are used in New England
boiled beef.*

Flavor

*They are tender and rich in
flavor if cooked slowly in
moist heat.*

Also known as

Short plate ribs.

Substitute

Back ribs.

Loin

The loin primal is one of the middle meats of the beef animal or carcass and includes the thirteenth rib and backbone. It consists of the short loin and the strip loin.

The primal weighs around 40 pounds and is taken from the area between the rib and sirloin primals. The quality of the loin—and particularly the marbling within it—is often used to gauge the grade of the entire animal. Loin cuts can be bone-in or boneless. They are expensive and are often reserved for special occasions. The front portion of the smaller, pointed tenderloin lies parallel to the loin.

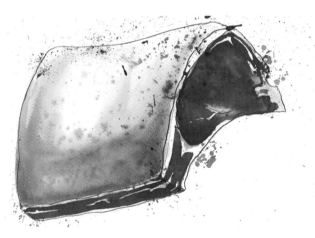

Flavor

Loin cuts can be incredibly tender and flavorsome, with a dense grain. Cuts with the most marbling are particularly succulent and tender—the loin can be a little chewy if the marbling is insufficient—and cuts from the rib end are generally the most tender. Whole loins are often dry-aged by hanging.

Also known as

Diamond cut, short loin, shell loin, short-cut beef, strip loin, and top loin.

Cooking

To retain optimum texture and flavor, the loin is best cooked rare or medium-rare. Loin roasts are roasted; steaks are best suited to frying or grilling.

Top loin steak

The top loin steak comes from the top of the loin section and can be bone-in or boneless.

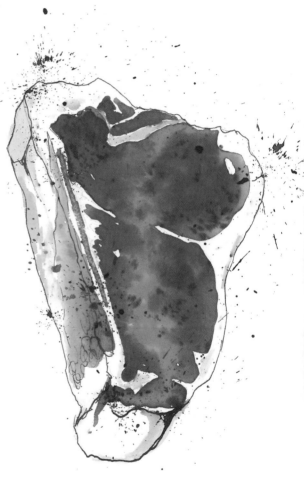

Flavor

The top loin steak is tender and flavorful.

Cooking

It requires hot, fast cooking, such as frying or grilling. It is best served rare or medium-rare.

Also known as

New York strip steak, Ambassador steak, boneless club steak, hotel-style steak, Kansas City steak, strip loin steak, veiny steak, shell steak, and faux filet *(French).*

T-bone steak

The T-bone steak is cut from the front section of the loin, next to the ribs. The steak includes a section of the tenderloin and strip loin. It takes its name from the T-shaped bone that runs through the center of the meat.

Flavor

T-bone steak is incredibly tender and flavorful.

Cooking

It is best fried or grilled until rare or medium-rare.

Also known as

Bistecca alla fiorentina in Tuscany, where it is large enough to be shared between two people.

Substitute

Porterhouse steak.

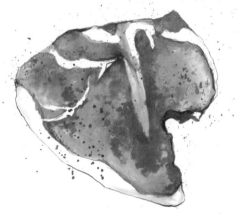

Flavor

The porterhouse steak is tender and full of flavor.

Porterhouse steak

The porterhouse steak is cut from the middle section of the loin. Like the T-bone steak it contains the T-shaped bone, but it consists of a larger section of the tenderloin and the strip loin and consequently commands a higher price than the T-bone steak. There are strict guidelines as to how large the tenderloin section of the steak must be for the steak to be classed as porterhouse.

Cooking

It is best fried or grilled until rare or medium-rare.

Substitute

T-bone steak.

Tenderloin roast and steak

The tenderloin roast is cut from the long pointed section called the tenderloin, which lies alongside the loin. It is expensive but good value because there is little or no wastage. The roast ranks as number one in tenderness of all the cuts from the beef carcass. The roast can be cut into steaks or thinly sliced for the classic Italian dish, carpaccio.

Flavor

Because it is an inner muscle that is rarely worked or exercised, the tenderloin has a delicately mellow flavor and a meltingly tender texture.

Cooking

It requires minimal preparation, although some recipes call for it to be stuffed. It cooks quickly and can be fried, grilled, or roasted. Tenderloin steaks can be grilled, broiled, or fried.

Also known as

Filet steak, fillet of beef; bifteck, filet, *and* filet mignon *(French). Tenderloin steaks are also known as* tournedos *(French). A thick steak cut from here is known as* Châteaubriand *in France.*

Chain

This is largely gristle which runs along the length of the tenderloin and has hardly any meat on it. It can sometimes be sold with the tenderloin. The chain can be cut into steaks and is fairly expensive but there is little or no wastage.

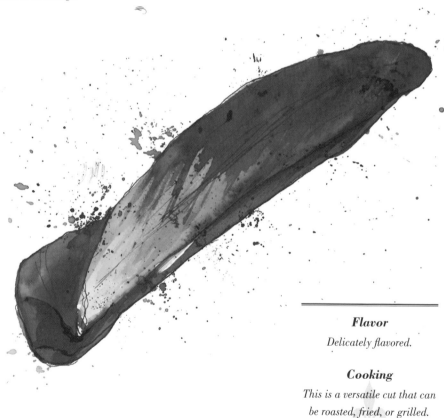

Flavor
Delicately flavored.

Cooking
This is a versatile cut that can be roasted, fried, or grilled.

Also known as
Rope, bavette, and chaînette (French).

Sirloin

The sirloin primal is taken from the upper hip of the beef animal or carcass. It weighs around 22 pounds and is one of the middle meats. It is less tender than the loin and rib primals and is therefore a cheaper cut.

The sirloin can be divided into the top sirloin butt—the stub end of the tenderloin—and the bottom sirloin butt. Sometimes part of the bottom sirloin can be included in the round primal, in which case it is known as the sirloin tip. Most cuts from the sirloin are full flavored, although their texture can vary in terms of tenderness depending from where exactly in the primal they have been taken.

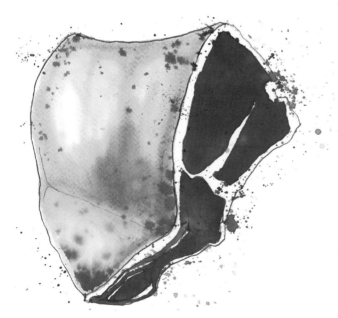

Flavor

The top sirloin butt is favored over the bottom sirloin; it is worked less by the animal and is less tough. Cuts can be bone-in or boneless. A sirloin steak with fine, even marbling can sometimes be as tender as a fillet steak.

Cooking

Some sirloin cuts are suitable only for stewing or braising, while others offer tender steaks for flash-frying. Sirloin is also used for ground beef. Two sirloins roasted together (sometimes with the round) are known as a baron of beef.

Tri-tip roast and tri-tip steak

This is a curved, triangular-shaped cut taken from the bottom of the sirloin. It is boneless, relatively inexpensive, and offers excellent value for money as there is little wastage. Tri-tip steaks are cut from the tri-tip roast.

Flavor

The tri-tip roast contains little fat and can provide great tenderness and a robust flavor.

Cooking

It responds well to marinades and strong flavors. The roast can be grilled, broiled, or roasted. Allow the top fat to melt into the meat as it roasts. Leftovers are great sliced and served cold in sandwiches the next day. Tri-tip steaks are great for barbecuing, broiling, or frying and are particularly popular in California.

Also known as

Corner cut, knuckle cap, Santa Maria barbecue, sirloin triangle muscle, triangle roast, and triangle tip. Tri-tip steaks are also known as triangle steaks.

Top sirloin roast

The top sirloin roast is usually sold boneless, though it can also be bone-in. It is more tender than the bottom sirloin as it is worked less by the animal, and is a great-value choice for feeding a crowd. It is one of the cuts often used in London Broil.

Flavor

Top sirloin roast is less expensive than a rib roast but just as impressive and flavorful.

Cooking

Roasting allows the top fat to melt over and baste the meat as it cooks.

Also known as

Center cut sirloin roast, top sirloin butt, head loin, hip sirloin, and coulotte *(French).*

Substitute

Rib-eye roast or rib roast.

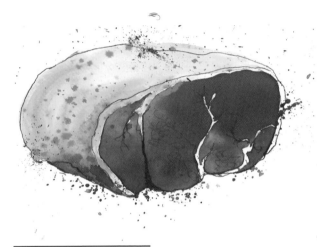

Flavor

Great for grilling or frying.

Also known as

Petite top sirloin steak and sirloin butt steak. A thick-cut top sirloin steak is also known as Châteaubriand *(although in France the* Châteaubriand *is cut from the tenderloin).*

Top sirloin steak

This is a boneless steak cut from the top sirloin. Some top sirloin steaks can be mouthwateringly juicy and full of flavor.

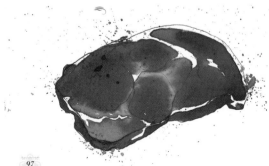

Round

Weighing around 80 pounds, the round is only slightly smaller than the chuck primal. It is one of the end meats and is taken from the top of the hind leg of the beef animal or carcass, continuing down toward the shank.

The round is divided into knuckle, top round, and bottom round and contains a section of the aitchbone (hipbone). Cuts from certain parts of the round (including the sirloin) are known as rump. Beef rolls, beef olives, *involtini* (Italian), and *roulade* (French) are cut from the round. These are tough, thin cuts which are pounded, stuffed, rolled, and then braised, usually in a rich sauce.

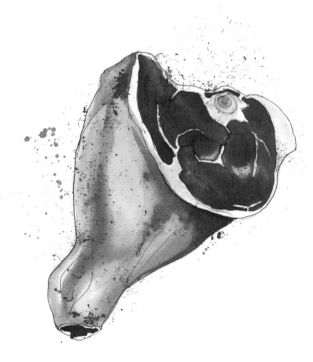

Flavor

Meat cut from the round is lean and not especially tender, particularly the parts closer to the ground, which are exercised more and are consequently tough.

Cooking

Round cuts are generally suited to slow, moist cooking methods, such as pot-roasting, which break down the connective tissue and bring out the flavor. Round can also be dried out and smoked to make beef jerky.

Top round

The top round is a lean roast from which thick steaks are cut. It is cut
from the upper, inner thigh and is therefore the most tender part of the
round. It is one of the cuts often used in London Broil.

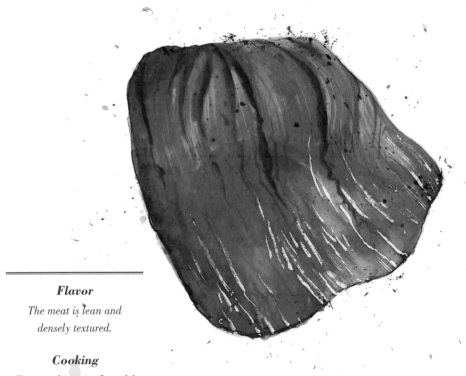

Flavor

*The meat is lean and
densely textured.*

Cooking

*Top round is quite flavorful
but requires marinating before
cooking to tenderize it. It is
best suited to pot-roasting.*

Substitutes

Flank steak.

Flavor

*This can be a flavorful cut
if cooked correctly.*

Cooking

Bottom round

....

Bottom round is the lowest part of the round cut. It is taken from the
outside of the leg and, as it is the most exercised, the meat is relatively
tough and contains a lot of connective tissue. The bottom round can be
further divided into eye of round, the flat, and the heel. Bottom round
cuts are best braised or cooked slowly in liquid to tenderize them. The
heel is a boneless cut and is the toughest of all the bottom round cuts.
Cuts from the bottom round can be known as rump.

*Bottom round demands slow,
moist cooking in order to
tenderize it and for the flavor
to be released. It is often cut
up for stewing and used as
kabob meat.*

Also known as

*Manhattan roast and steak,
Swiss steak, silverside, and
breakfast steak.*

Eye of round roast and eye of round steak

The eye of round, which sits in the middle of the round, is generally a tough cut.

Flavor

With correct cooking, this can be a deliciously flavorful cut.

Cooking

Eye of round roasts and steaks require slow, moist cooking, such as braising or pot-roasting. Steaks benefit from being marinated before being broiled, grilled, or braised.

Also known as

Breakfast steak and sandwich steak.

Substitute

Round tip roast or round tip steak.

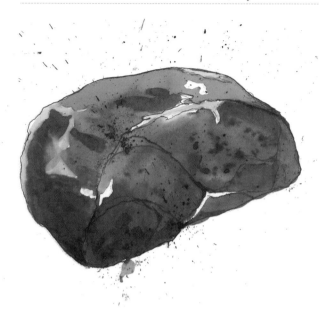

Flavor

Round tip roast is less tough than roasts cut from other round cuts.

Cooking

It can be roasted but is often braised or cut up into stewing steak.

Also known as

Ball tip roast and steak, trimmed tip steak (if the cut has been trimmed), sirloin tip steak, breakfast steak, knuckle steak, tip center steak, and round peeled knuckle.

Substitute

Eye of round roast or eye of round steak.

Round tip roast and round tip steak

Round tip steaks are cut from the round tip roast.

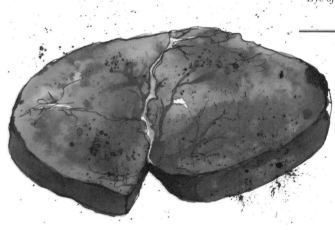

Sirloin tip center roast and sirloin tip center steak

The sirloin tip center is a simple, economical cut which makes a quick and easy roast, or may be made into stewing meat, cut into strips for stir-frying, or ground.

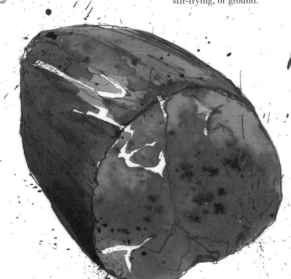

Flavor
Lean and tender with good flavor.

Cooking
Benefits from marinating. Best suited to roasting, frying, or broiling to medium-rare.

Sirloin tip side steak

This is a relatively new and economical steak. Although it is classed as part of the round, it is technically the very end of the sirloin.

Flavor

The sirloin tip side steak is a boneless, lean cut. It is less tender than the tip center steak.

Cooking

It requires marinating before being grilled or fried.

Flavor

Meat from the knuckle is less tender than that from the sirloin but it has excellent flavor. The most tender part is the center of the knuckle.

Cooking

The knuckle is best suited to roasting. Slightly tougher steaks cut from the knuckle are nevertheless tasty and are often cut into thin strips or slices.

Also known as

Sirloin butt roast, breakfast steak, minute steak, and sandwich steak.

Knuckle

The knuckle is cut from the top of the round, just behind the sirloin. It is a versatile boneless cut that can be divided into roasts and steaks. Strips of meat for the Russian dish Stroganoff are often cut from the knuckle.

Shank

The shank primal is a basic cut that is taken from the fore or rear leg of the carcass and has a bone running through its center. The rear shank is considered to be part of the round.

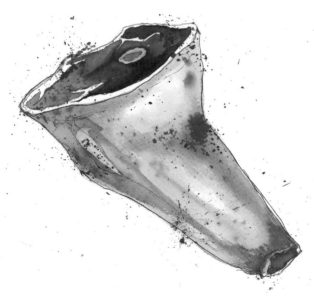

Flavor

Shank is a relatively lean cut and is really flavorsome. It is naturally tough with plenty of gelatin-rich connective tissue. The rear shank has little culinary value as it is particularly tough.

Cooking

Fore and rear shanks can be cooked whole and are suitable for long, slow stewing to tenderize the meat. They can also be ground and used in processed meat products.

Also known as

The hind leg is known as leg of beef and the fore leg is known as shin (British).

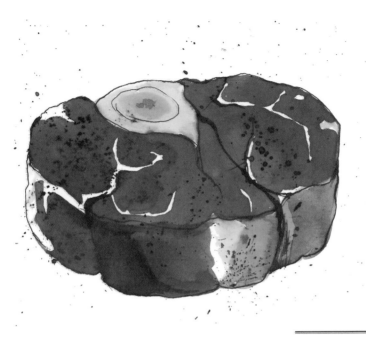

Flavor

This is a rich and flavorsome cut.

Shank cross-cut

Shank cross-cut is cut across the shank and therefore contains a round piece of the leg bone in the center.

Cooking

Shank cross-cuts require slow, moist cooking in liquid and are therefore ideal for stewing or simmering in a stock until the meat falls away from the bone. The stock can then be turned into a delicious beef soup, combined with the shredded meat.

Variety meats

Variety meats are cuts taken from the extremities of the animal or the organs within. They are also known as offal or innards.

Brains

Cows' brains are taken from the front of the skull. They are a popular delicacy in France, although following the BSE outbreak, they are no longer available in some countries. Cows' brains should be plump and firm. To prepare, soak in salted water then rinse and remove the membrane and any blood vessels. Poach whole or slice and fry in butter until tender and serve sprinkled with lemon juice and chopped herbs.

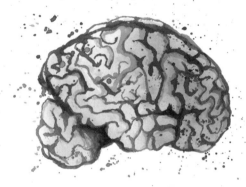

Tongue

A tongue from a beef carcass is long and flat and larger than you might imagine. To prepare, soak in water, then poach in a light stock until tender. Remove the inedibly tough skin before eating. Tongue is often served cold, usually jellied and pressed ready to be sliced.

Cheeks

Beef cheeks are taken from the
cheek area of the head of the
beef carcass. To prepare, trim
away gristle, then season and
brown until golden. Cheeks are
naturally tough but the dense,
lean meat becomes meltingly
tender with slow, moist cooking,
such as braising. They can also
be marinated and stuffed before
being cooked.

Heart

A fresh heart from a cow is bright
red and firm. It is a naturally
muscular organ, cheap to buy,
and flavorful when cooked. The
older the animal, the tougher
the heart and the longer it will
require braising, stewing, or slow-
roasting to tenderize it. A tender
heart from a younger animal can
be sliced and fried or cut into
cubes, threaded onto skewers,
and broiled.

Tripe

Tripe is the lining taken from one of the cow's four stomachs, though only that from the first three stomachs is used for culinary purposes. Tripe has a characteristic spongelike or honeycomb appearance and texture. It is usually boiled in salted water or stock, then stewed or braised. It can then be marinated before being fried or broiled. Blanket tripe—also known as double tripe—is taken from the first, largest stomach and is smoother than tripe taken from the second and third stomachs.

Sweetbreads

Sweetbreads is the culinary name given both to the thymus gland in the throat and the pancreas in the stomach of the cow. Both types of sweetbread are delicately flavored and they can be prepared in the same way—by poaching briefly in water or a light stock. They can then be dusted with flour and fried until hot and creamy inside or they can be roasted or braised.

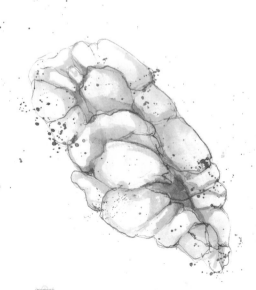

Liver

Cows' liver has a strong flavor
and is tougher and cheaper to
buy than calves' liver. Liver from
these older animals requires
braising or stewing to tenderize it.

Kidneys

To prepare kidneys, first remove
the central fatty core, the outer
membrane, and any blood vessels,
then rinse in cold water. Cows'
kidneys can be relatively tough,
and require slow, moist cooking
such as braising or stewing.

Oxtail

Oxtail is the name given to the
tail from any type of beef cattle.
It is sold cut into pieces and,
while meaty, it is also bony, and
contains plenty of connective
tissue that breaks down into a
gelatinous liquid during slow
cooking, such as braising. Oxtail
soup is a richly flavored dish,
popular in Great Britain.

Testicles

Bulls' testicles are known as
fries and are served as a delicacy
in certain parts of Europe. To
prepare, blanch them in boiling
water, refresh, then remove the
skin. They can then be marinated
and sliced into pieces, floured,
and fried, and are particularly
tasty served with a lemon- or
vinegar-based dressing and
freshly chopped herbs.

Udder

The udder is the mammary
gland of the cow and, although
seldom used in cooking today, it
was particularly popular in the
Middle Ages. It can be sliced and
soaked in cold water, before being
blanched, then braised or roasted.
Udder is a fatty meat that can
also be finely ground and used
in forcemeat (a smooth stuffing),
pâtés, and terrines.

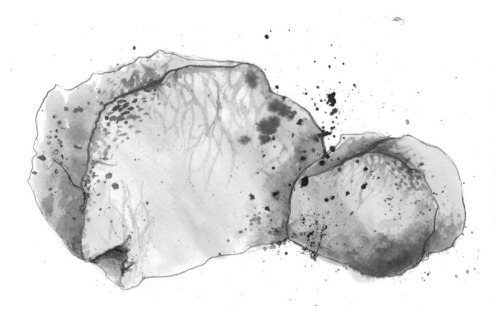

Beef bones

Bones from the leg, knuckle, or neck vertebrae are rich in connective
tissue and are useful for flavoring and adding texture to stocks, broths,
and gravies. They are sometimes known as bouillon bones and can be
acquired cheaply from a butcher or can be taken from a cooked roast.
For a flavorsome beef stock, roast beef bones until golden. Add to a pan
of cold water with herbs and chopped vegetables and simmer into a rich
stock. Beef bones containing marrow will yield gelatin, adding extra
flavor and texture. Bones are an excellent conductor of heat and lend a
great flavor to bone-in roasts.

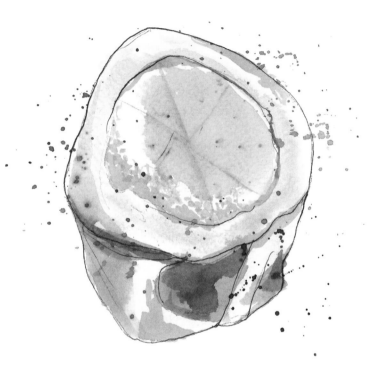

Marrow

Bone marrow is the soft, fatty tissue found in the hollow cavities of the leg and thigh bones of a cow carcass. It is cooked in the bone, usually by poaching. A marrow bone added to a stock pot will lend a gelatinous, silky texture and a deep flavor. Beef marrow can also be served as a delicacy in the bone it was cooked in, with a teaspoon or small scoop to pick it from the bone before spreading it onto bread or toast.

Veal

Veal is the meat from a calf slaughtered up to the age of 12 months. The production of veal is closely linked to the dairy industry. In order to produce milk, cows must produce calves. Female calves are raised for the dairy industry; males are slaughtered for their meat.

There are various methods of farming veal calves, each affecting the outcome of the meat. Some veal calves are removed from their mothers at birth, kept indoors, fed only milk, and slaughtered before they are one month old. Meat from these calves is pale and tender. Others are allowed more freedom outdoors. They exist on a diet of hay and grain and are kept alive for longer. Meat from calves raised in this way is firmer-textured and darker in color.

While veal cuts can be incredibly tender, they have less fat and marbling than beef and therefore often require slower cooking. When buying veal, choose cuts that are firm and dry without too much outside fat.

Shoulder and blade

The shoulder and blade primal of the veal carcass is cut from the same area as the chuck primal of the beef animal. It includes the first four ribs and the neck. The shoulder and blade is somewhat tougher and less tender than the veal leg, though it has great flavor when roasted or stewed. The veal shoulder can be cut into the point or flat cut, comparable to the brisket primal of the beef animal. The point is a smaller, fattier cut than the larger, leaner flat cut. Neck of veal is an economical cut, yet tougher still than the shoulder; it is best suited to stewing or grinding into hamburgers.

Veal shoulder arm roast

This cut contains the arm bone and rib bone. It is best suited to braising or roasting.

Veal shoulder blade roast

This cut contains the blade bone, ribs, and part of the backbone. It is best suited to braising or roasting or can also be sliced into steaks for braising, frying, or broiling.

Center leg roast

This cut is incredibly tender. It can be bone-in or boned, then stuffed, rolled, and roasted. Also known as leg center cut and leg roast. Steaks can be cut from the center leg roast. Feet are used for flavoring stocks and stews. They contain a small amount of meat and are rich in gelatin, adding a delectable texture and richness to stews.

Veal shank

This is cut from the leg. It can be braised or pot-roasted whole or sliced through the bone for Italy's famous dish osso buco—"osso" meaning bone and "buco" hole. The marrow from the bone can be picked out with a toothpick or other small utensil.

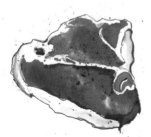

Leg or round

The leg or round is sometimes known as hind-saddle of veal. The leg cut usually includes the sirloin (although the sirloin is sometimes included in the loin primal), the rump, and the hind-shank. Cuts from the leg and round are great for roasting or braising—either boned or bone-in—and can be cut into cutlets or tender boneless slices. Leg cuts are also known as *escalope de veau* (French), sirloin chop, sirloin steak, and *Schnitzel* (Germany and Austria). Roasts are also known as eye of round roast, rump roast, sirloin roast, and top round roast.

Veal cutlets

These are taken from the center of the top round and contain some of the marrow bone. Veal birds are cut from the eye of the cutlet. These tender cuts are pounded and rolled and are best suited to frying or broiling.

Scaloppine

This is a thin cut from the center of the leg (or sometimes the loin). It should be cut to order, pounded flat, then fried.

Sirloin of veal

This cut is often classed as part of the leg primal. It can be cut into roasts—a bone-in standing sirloin roast (also known as rump roast) and a boned rolled double sirloin roast (also known as double rump roast). The sirloin can also be cut into chops and steaks.

Breast and rib

The breast and rib primal contains the rack and ribs 6 through 12. The breast, taken from the underside of the rib, can contain the lower ribs or can be cut into a boneless roast. Although it has great flavor, it is a relatively tough, slightly fatty cut. It is best suited to slow, moist cooking such as braising or slow-roasting. Cuts from the breast are also known as flank and *poitrine de veau* (French).

Crown roast of veal

This is made by curving and tying the ribs together into a circle or crown shape. The crown is usually stuffed before being roasted and is often served as a splendid centerpiece at elegant celebrations.

Veal hotel rack

This contains the rib bones or can be boned into a veal rack rib-eye. It is succulent and flavorsome and can be cut into veal rack rib chops. If the meat is cut away to expose the bone, the chop is known as a Frenched rib chop.

Short ribs

These are taken from the rib roast and can be braised like beef short ribs.

Loin

The veal loin lies between the rib section and the sirloin (upper hip). It is sold in two sections—the short and the butt—and also includes the tenderloin. Cuts from the loin are expensive, tender, and can be cut into small bone-in or boneless roasts, chops, steaks, and cutlets. The kidneys and sirloin are sometimes included in the loin primal (although the sirloin can also be included in the leg primal). Thin, boneless slices known as scaloppine can be cut from the loin.

Loin roast of veal

This contains the T-shaped bones and can be cut into T-bone chops, which include part of the eye and the tenderloin. These are best grilled or roasted.

Loin roast

This is a bone-in roast. If the bones are removed, it is known as a rolled loin roast and can be stuffed, rolled, and tied.

Veal tenderloin

This cut lies beneath the ribs. It is a tender cut for roasting or can be sliced into medallions for veal saltimbocca, a dish that involves wrapping medallions of veal with prosciutto, sage, and lemon and frying in butter and wine. Tenderloin is also known as short tenderloin, veal tender, and filet (French).

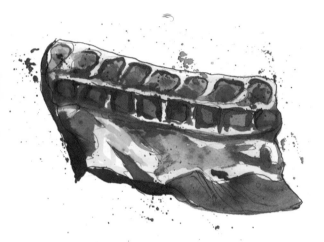

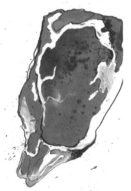

Loin veal chops

These are similar to loin chops but traditionally include a slice of kidney, often skewered in place. They are best suited to roasting, grilling, or broiling.

Variety veal

Veal brains

These are creamy and delicately flavored. They are a particularly popular delicacy in Europe.

Variety meats from the veal calf are incredibly tender and they are the most highly valued of all animal variety meats.

Veal cheeks

These come from the cheek part of the calf's head and are similar to beef cheeks. They are best suited to braising and slow-roasting.

Veal kidneys

These should be plump and mild-smelling. They are more delicately flavored than beef kidneys and are naturally tender. They can be fried, grilled, or broiled, whole or sliced, until just pink inside (they can become a little tough if overcooked).

Veal head

This can be cooked and presented in numerous and elaborate ways. Also known as tête de veau *(French), it is usually poached or braised and sliced into broths or used in terrines and pies.*

Veal sweetbreads

These are similar in texture to veal brains. As with beef, sweetbreads is the culinary name given to the thymus gland in the throat and the pancreas in the stomach of the veal calf. Delicately flavored, veal sweetbreads are an expensive choice but are delicious poached, then dusted in flour and fried in butter.

Veal tongue

This is smaller and less tough than beef tongue. It is best braised or poached.

Calves' liver

This is pale pink and. compared with liver from other animals, it is mildly flavored. It has an incredibly smooth texture and can vary in appearance, from pale to dark in color, depending on how the animal was reared. It can be fried in butter, broiled until tender, or wrapped in bacon and roasted.

Beef products

Corned beef

Corned beef is made by curing brisket or flank. Sometimes chuck, or
the leaner cut silverside (from the bottom round), is used. The "corn"
refers to the grains of salt used in the brine in which the meat is
cured, before being poached in water on the stovetop or in the oven.
It can then be pot-roasted and is traditionally served with mustard,
vegetables, and boiled potatoes. Leftovers can be thinly sliced and
served cold in rye bread sandwiches with mustard and pickles. Corned
beef is known as salt beef in Great Britain.

Dried and smoked beef

Jerky originated in South Africa. It is made by salting and air-drying a variety of meat, such as beef or game. Jerky is almost black in color, can be stored at room temperature, and is tough and chewy to eat. It is also known as jerked beef or biltong.

Bresaola is an Italian delicacy made from cuts of beef taken from the round that are cured with salt, then air-dried. It is cut into wafer-thin slices and should be moist and delicately flavored.

Pastrami is made from smoked corned beef. It is often served cold in sandwiches, though can also be served hot with vegetables.

Suet

Suet is the hard white fat taken from around a cow's kidneys. It was traditionally used for frying as it has a high smoking point; fish and chips in Great Britain were fried in suet until healthier oils became more popular. Suet is the fat used in suet pastry and in sweet and savory dumplings and puddings, including Christmas pudding and mincemeat. It is usually sold shredded—often dusted in flour to keep it from clumping together—or in blocks which need to be grated before being added to other ingredients.

Sausage

Sausages can be fresh, cured, dried, smoked, or precooked. There are numerous varieties; in Germany alone there are hundreds. Sausages can be made from any type of chopped or ground meat, which is often combined with fat, variety meats, and other fillers—depending on the quality of the sausage—then seasoned with herbs and spices. The mix is pushed into tubular casings, traditionally made from animal intestines, although now usually synthetic. Fresh sausages can be fried, grilled, roasted, or cooked in a stew or braise. A good-quality fresh sausage is firm, meaty, and well seasoned. Cured sausage, such as Italian or German salami, Spanish chorizo, and French saucisson can be made from beef. These do not need to be cooked and can be eaten cold. Black sausages—also known as black pudding—are made from blood and diced fat.

Techniques

How to fry a steak

A steak can be cooked from rare to well done. Timing is everything, and knowing how to cook a steak just as you like it is a useful skill to master. Piercing a steak with a meat thermometer is not advisable because it will let out all the flavorsome juices; neither is cutting into it to check before it is served, because it will spoil the presentation. The cooking time depends on the thickness of the steak, rather than its weight. Other factors such as the temperature and heat distribution of the pan and the temperature of the steak before it was added to the pan play a part too.

Recommended cooking times for frying
a ¾-inch-thick sirloin steak from room
temperature in a preheated pan are as follows:

Rare   1½ minutes per side
Medium-rare   2 minutes per side
Medium   2½ minutes per side
Well done   3½ minutes per side

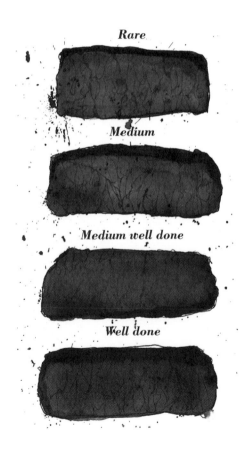

Rare

Medium

Medium well done

Well done

The cheek, chin, and forehead test

An accurate way to test for doneness is to press the steak lightly with your fingertip and compare the way it feels to your cheek, chin, and forehead. A rare steak is soft and fleshy like your cheek; fleshy with some resistance, like your chin, is medium; firmer to the touch with more resistance, like your forehead, means it is well done.

The thumb test

Relax one hand and touch the fleshy part at the base of your thumb with your other index finger. It will feel soft and fleshy, like raw meat. Press the tip of your thumb against the tip of your forefinger on the same hand. Now feel the base of the thumb again. It will feel slightly tighter; this is like rare meat. Move your thumb from the forefinger to the middle finger, and the pad at the base of the thumb will feel a little tighter still; this is medium meat. Press your thumb against the tip of your fourth finger and it will tighten more; this is medium-to-well-done. Stretch the thumb to the little finger and the muscles in the base of the thumb will be tight and contracted, which is how well-done meat feels.

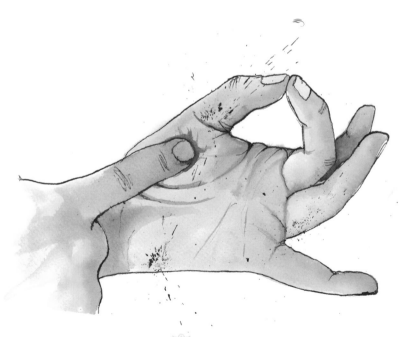

Meatballs

Meatballs can be made from ground beef, lamb, or pork, which is seasoned with salt and pepper and shaped into small balls. Freshly chopped herbs, such as parsley and rosemary, and diced onion can be added for extra flavor. Sometimes bread crumbs and beaten egg are added to bind the mixture together, though this is not strictly necessary, acting rather as a bulking agent and ultimately lessening the flavor and texture of the meatballs.

Using clean, wet hands, shape the seasoned ground meat into small balls (wetting your hands first will keep the meat from sticking to your fingers). Brown the meatballs in a large skillet until golden all over—this browning will enhance the final flavor of the dish. When sufficiently golden, add canned tomatoes or a tomato-based sauce, then cover and cook for at least 20 minutes until the meat is tender and cooked through. You can remove the lid for the last 10 minutes of cooking time to allow the sauce to reduce and thicken. Sprinkle with freshly chopped herbs and some grated cheese and serve with spaghetti.

Suet pastry

Suet—hard white beef fat—is most commonly used to make pastry. Suet pastry is made by mixing self-rising flour and half the amount of suet with just enough iced water to bind the mixture together to form a dough. If the suet is fresh, it should be chilled and grated into the dry ingredients and blended into the flour with fingertips. Adding too much water or overworking the dough will result in a tough pastry. The dough is then rolled out on a floured surface and used to line a buttered pudding basin. This can then be filled and topped with a suet pastry lid. To cook, the pudding is covered with waxed paper and foil, set into a pan of simmering water, and steamed until the filling is cooked through.

Carpaccio

Carpaccio is a classic dish that originated in Venice, Italy. Very fresh, raw beef fillet is placed in the freezer until just firm. It is then very thinly sliced, arranged on a plate, and dressed. There are many variations of the dressing but it often includes mayonnaise, vinegar, lemon juice, and mustard. The beef can be topped with chopped onions and capers. Sometimes a simple dressing of olive oil and balsamic vinegar is used and the dish is sprinkled with Parmesan cheese. Carpaccio is typically served as an appetizer rather than a main course. Today, the term carpaccio also refers to thinly sliced raw vegetables and fish.

Steak tartare

Steak tartare is a classic dish made from very fresh, finely chopped raw beef fillet seasoned with a combination of olive oil, lemon juice, French mustard, finely chopped onion, parsley, capers, gherkins, and plenty of salt and pepper. The mixture is pressed into a ring on the plate and topped with a raw egg or egg yolk (alternatively the raw egg can be stirred into the mixture). Sometimes the dish is assembled at the table by the waiter, and it is traditionally served with crisp French fries.

Chile-braised beef, New Mexican-style

Pieces of chuck, chiles, and bell peppers are braised together until tender in this New Mexican pot-roast. Enjoy shreds of the meat and peppers wrapped up in soft flour tortillas, with diced avocado, salsa, and sour cream on the side.

Serves 4–6

4–5 mild dried chile peppers
1 green bell pepper, seeded
and sliced
1 red bell pepper, seeded
and sliced
4 ripe tomatoes, diced
1 small to medium bunch
cilantro, chopped
5 garlic cloves, chopped
1 onion, chopped
2 fresh bay leaves
1½ tsp ground cumin
2–3 lb chuck steak or chuck
pot-roast, cut into 1-inch cubes
1 cup (8 fl oz) beef broth
1 cup (8 fl oz) English beer

Lightly toast the chiles over an open flame, then put them in a bowl. Cover with hot water and soak for at least 1 hour.

Preheat the oven to 350°F (180°C).

Discard the stems, skin, and seeds of the chiles and put half the flesh into a baking pan with half the bell peppers, tomatoes, cilantro, garlic, onion, bay leaves, and cumin. Top with the chuck, then layer over the remaining half of the ingredients. Season with salt, add the broth and beer, then cover tightly with foil.

Bake for 2 to 3 hours, adding more liquid if necessary, or until the chuck is tender. Remove the foil and bake for 30 minutes more, increasing the heat if necessary to brown and crisp the top. Serve hot.

Italian braised beef with onion and eggplant

This is the perfect prepare-ahead dinner or supper party dish, using beef shanks. It is perfect served with this simple vegetable stir-fry.

Serves 4

Preheat the oven to 325°F (170°C).

Mix together the flour and chili powder on a large plate. Add the shanks and turn to coat them in the flour mixture.

Heat 3 tbsp olive oil in a large flameproof, ovenproof dish. Add the floured shanks and brown well all over. Stir in the sliced garlic, oregano, tomatoes, and just enough broth to cover the meat. Bring to a boil, then cover and transfer to the oven. Bake for 3 hours or until the shanks are meltingly tender.

Heat the remaining oil in a hot skillet. Add the eggplant and fry until golden. Add the onion and fry for 3 minutes, then add the bell pepper and finely chopped garlic and stir-fry for 2 minutes.

Remove the shanks from the sauce, transfer to a plate, cover with foil, and keep warm. Add the stir-fried vegetables to the sauce and simmer, uncovered, for 5 to 10 minutes until the vegetables are tender and the sauce is well reduced.

Meanwhile, dry-fry the pancetta in the skillet until crisp.

To serve, divide the vegetables and sauce between four plates and top each with a shank. Spoon over the remaining sauce, then garnish with the pancetta and some chopped parsley.

2 tbsp all-purpose flour
1 tsp mild chili powder
4 beef shanks, each weighing
about 6 oz, trimmed
5 tbsp olive oil
2 large garlic cloves, sliced,
and 1 garlic clove,
finely chopped
2 tbsp chopped fresh oregano
1¾ cups (14 fl oz) canned
chopped tomatoes
2 cups (16 fl oz) beef or
vegetable broth
2 medium eggplants, cut
into 2-inch chunks
1 large onion, cut into sixths
1 red onion, cut into sixths
1 red bell pepper, seeded
and diced
8 slices pancetta or very
thin bacon
Chopped parsley, to garnish

Old-fashioned pot-roast with onion gravy

There are many recipes for pot-roast—all of which involve browning a large cut of beef, then adding a splash of liquid to the pot and cooking it slowly. This delightfully old-fashioned recipe uses tomato juice to moisten the meat, keeping it tender and making a flavorsome gravy.

Serves 8–10

*5–6 lb brisket point
cut, trimmed*

1 tbsp all-purpose flour

4 tbsp vegetable oil

*6 onions, cut into
½-inch rings*

*4–6 garlic cloves,
finely chopped*

1 cup (8 fl oz) tomato juice

½ tsp dried thyme

½ tsp paprika

1 bay leaf

*6 carrots, cut into ¼-inch
slices on the diagonal*

Parsley sprigs, to garnish

Rinse the brisket under cold running water and pat dry with paper towels. Put onto a plate and dust with flour. Heat 2 tbsp oil in a large flameproof, ovenproof dish. Add the brisket and cook for 5 to 7 minutes until browned on the underside. Turn and cook for 5 to 6 minutes until browned. Transfer to a plate.

Preheat the oven to 325°F (170°C).

Add the remaining oil to the dish. Stir in the onions and cook until softened. Add the garlic and cook for 1 minute, then add the tomato juice, scraping any bits from the bottom of the dish. Add the thyme, paprika, and bay leaf and season with salt and pepper.

Return the brisket to the dish with enough water to cover all the ingredients. Bring to a boil, skimming off any foam from the surface. Cover tightly and bake in the oven for 3 hours or until the brisket is tender. Add the carrots and cook for 30 minutes more, or until tender.

If the sauce is quite thin, remove the brisket to a serving platter to keep warm. Put the dish on the stove and bubble until the sauce is reduced and thickened. Carve the brisket into ¼-inch-thick slices, then divide between four plates. Spoon over the sauce and garnish with parsley.

Braised beef with white radish

Cooking this Korean casserole slowly will result in a rich, thick sauce that will coat the ribs and radish. The tasty ribs will add lots of flavor to the dish.

Serves 4

Make a few deep slashes in a lattice pattern on the meaty side of each rib, then add to a large saucepan of boiling water. Return to a boil, simmer for 1 minute, then drain and rinse the ribs under cold water.

Put the ribs and white radish in a large skillet with 2 cups (16 fl oz) water and bring to a boil. Cover and simmer gently for 40 minutes.

Meanwhile, soak the Chinese mushrooms in hot water for 20 minutes. Remove with a slotted spoon and cut away any hard parts, including the stems.

Add the garlic, soy sauce, toasted sesame oil and seeds, sugar, and plenty of freshly ground black pepper to the ribs. Return to a boil, then lower the heat and cook, partly covered, for 20 minutes.

Add the mushrooms and cook, stirring occasionally, for 30 minutes or until the ribs are tender. Remove the lid, raise the heat, and bubble until the sauce is reduced to a few spoonfuls. Serve with rice and steamed green vegetables.

3 lb beef back ribs, cut into
2-inch segments
1 lb white radish, cut into
2-inch cubes
8 dried Chinese
black mushrooms
4–6 garlic cloves, crushed
5 tbsp soy sauce
1 tbsp toasted sesame oil
2 tbsp toasted sesame seeds
2 tbsp light brown sugar

Hanging steak

This steak, also called boxeater or back roll, can sometimes be hard to find, so ask your butcher to order it in. The dark meat is exceptionally juicy and has a sublime flavor.

Serves 4

Preheat the broiler or barbecue.

4 hanging steaks
Olive oil, for brushing
Lemon zest, to garnish

Remove all fat and sinew from the steaks, rinse, and pat dry with paper towels. Remove the center sheet of gristle from each steak and cut each into two pieces.

Brush the steaks with oil, and season. Cook under the broiler or on the barbecue, turning frequently, so they cook evenly all over—this will take about 4–5 minutes under a broiler, or 10 minutes on the barbecue. Take care not to cook beyond medium or they will become tough.

Carve into slices against the grain, sprinkle with the lemon zest, and serve with boiled or baked potatoes and a salad.

Cuban beef with peppers and spices

This hearty Cuban dish is known as *vaca frita*. Flank steak is full of flavor, and the leftovers are great in sandwiches with mayonnaise and mustard. The cooking liquid can be strained and reserved for soup.

Serves 6

Put the flank steak in a pot with one-third of the onion, the carrot, one-third of the garlic, the bouillon cubes, and enough water to cover. Bring to a boil, then simmer over a very low heat, adding more water to keep the meat covered. Cook for 1½ to 2 hours, then let cool in the liquid.

Remove the beef from the liquid. Shred it into a bowl, season with salt and pepper, then toss with two-thirds of the lime juice, the cumin seeds, chili powder, and oregano.

Heat 1–2 tbsp olive oil in a heavy nonstick skillet. Add about half of the remaining onion and fry until soft. Season with salt and set aside. Fry the bell peppers in a little oil until softened, then set aside.

To make the salsa, put the remaining garlic into a bowl and mix in the remaining onion and lime juice, the tomatoes, cilantro, and green chile. Set aside.

Heat 1–2 tbsp olive oil in the skillet. Add the meat mixture in batches and sauté for 5 minutes over a high heat until browned. Repeat until all the meat is crisp and browned. Return the fried onions and peppers to the pan, mix well, and serve with the salsa, lime wedges, sour cream, and scallions.

2 lb flank steak
3 onions, thinly sliced
1 carrot, chopped
6–8 garlic cloves, chopped
1–2 beef bouillon cubes
¼–½ cup (2–4 fl oz) lime juice
½ tsp cumin seeds
½ tsp mild chili powder
½ tsp dried oregano
¼ cup (2 fl oz) extra-virgin olive oil
1 green bell pepper, seeded and chopped
1 red bell pepper, seeded and chopped
2 ripe tomatoes, diced
5 tbsp chopped cilantro
1–2 fresh green chile peppers, chopped
Wedges of lime, sour cream, and thinly sliced scallions, to serve

Prosciutto tournedos

Wrapping prosciutto around the steak gives the meat a wonderful Italian flavor. Cuts from the tenderloin are particularly tender and require little in the way of cooking or preparation.

Serves 4

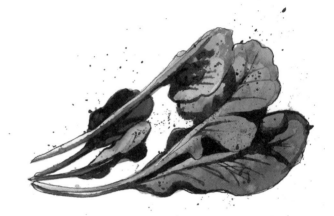

½ lb spinach
¼ tsp grated nutmeg
¼ cup (2 oz) ricotta cheese
4 slices bread
A little butter or olive oil,
for frying
4 slices prosciutto
4 tenderloin steaks
or medallions, each
weighing 4 oz
2 tomatoes, halved

Bring a pan of water to a boil and cook the spinach for 2 minutes. Drain, pressing out any excess water, then mix with the nutmeg and ricotta. Season with salt and pepper.

Cut out a round of bread from each slice, discarding the crusts, then fry on both sides in the butter or olive oil until golden. Transfer to a serving plate and spoon the spinach mixture on top. Set aside in a warm place.

Cut the prosciutto into strips the same width as the steaks. Wind the strips firmly around the steaks, season, then broil or fry until golden. Serve on top of the spinach mixture and top each with half a tomato.

Steak bordelaise

For the best texture and flavor choose well-marbled sirloin steaks. The bordelaise sauce can be made with red or white wine—go for whichever you're drinking.

Serves 4

To make the sauce, put the shallot into a small pan with 4 tbsp butter and 2 tbsp water and simmer until the water has evaporated and the shallot starts to fry—take care that it does not brown.

Add the wine, bring to a boil, and reduce by two-thirds. Add the broth and remaining butter, then bring to a boil. Simmer until thickened, then add the parsley. Mix well, season to taste, and set aside.

Heat a large skillet until very hot. Add the steaks—in batches if necessary—and cook to your preference. Remove from the pan and keep warm. Add the sauce to the skillet, stirring into the pan juices and bubble for 1 minute until hot.

Divide the steaks between four plates, spoon over the sauce, and garnish with parsley.

4 tbsp finely chopped shallot
6 tbsp unsalted butter
½ cup (4 fl oz) red or
white wine
½ cup (4 fl oz) beef broth
2 tbsp chopped parsley, plus
extra to garnish
Four 8-oz sirloin steaks

Warm shredded beef salad

This slightly sweet dressing, together with the caramelized strips of beef, make a mouthwatering salad.

Serves 4

3 tbsp soy sauce

1 tbsp sweet sherry

½ tsp ground mixed peppercorns

¼ tsp chili powder

1 tsp honey

1½ lb sirloin steaks, trimmed and cut into thin strips

A handful of mixed salad leaves

1 tbsp mirin

1 tbsp peanut oil, plus 2 tsp

1 tsp rice wine vinegar

1 tsp toasted sesame oil

2 tsp cornstarch, sieved

¼ tsp salt

4 scallions, sliced on the diagonal

Sesame seeds, to garnish

To make the marinade, mix together the soy sauce, sherry, ground peppercorns, chili powder, and honey in a shallow dish. Add the beef and turn to coat. Marinate for 30 minutes.

Put the salad leaves in a bowl. Mix together the mirin, 1 tbsp peanut oil, and the rice wine vinegar, then drizzle over the leaves.

Drain the beef and pat dry on paper towels. Add the toasted sesame oil and 2 tsp peanut oil to a wok or skillet. Sprinkle the cornstarch and salt over the beef, then immediately add to the hot pan. Stir-fry over a high heat until crisp, then spoon onto the salad.

Mix well, sprinkle with the scallions, and serve warm, garnished with sesame seeds.

Beef Stroganoff

Beef knuckle gives this dish a wonderful, rich flavor, and simmering the mushrooms in the wine adds a delightful piquancy. Plain noodles are the best accompaniment.

Serves 4

Put the beef slices between two sheets of nonstick parchment paper and beat with a tenderizer to thin them out. Slice into 1-inch wide strips.

Melt the butter in a large, heavy skillet. Quickly sauté the beef, turning it regularly to brown it lightly all over. Season, then remove with a slotted spoon and set aside.

Add the onion to the buttery juices in the pan and cook, stirring, until soft. Add the mushrooms and cook until golden, 5–10 minutes. Add the paprika, nutmeg, and wine, bring to a boil, then simmer until the liquid has reduced to one quarter of the original amount.

Add the sour cream and simmer to a thick coating consistency. Return the meat to the pan and return to a simmer. Serve with noodles.

1½ lb beef knuckle, cut into
½-inch slices
6 tbsp butter
1 medium onion, chopped
12 oz mushrooms, sliced
2 tsp paprika
2 pinches of ground nutmeg
4 tbsp white wine
1 cup (8 fl oz) sour cream

Steak au poivre

This is just one version of this timelessly popular dish. Marinating the steak enables the pepper flavor to penetrate the meat, while the cream cools its heat.

Serves 4

Sprinkle 2 tsp pepper and the garlic over one side of the steaks and press well in. Leave for 30 minutes.

Brush a ridged griddle pan with oil and heat until almost smoking. Add the steaks—in batches if necessary—peppered-side down, and cook to your preference, turning once. Remove the steaks from the pan and set aside to keep warm.

3 tsp ground black pepper
2 garlic cloves, crushed
Four 8-oz top round steaks
a little oil, for brushing
½ cup (4 fl oz) brandy
2 tbsp butter
1 cup (8 fl oz) half and half
½ cup (4 fl oz) crème fraîche
or sour cream
1 tsp beef glaze or
stock (optional)

Meanwhile, put the brandy, butter, and remaining pepper into a large skillet. Heat to melt the butter and reduce the liquid to 1 tbsp. Add the cream, crème fraîche, and beef glaze or stock, if using. Bring to a simmer, then reduce to a light coating consistency.

Add the steaks, peppered-side up, to the skillet. Bubble for 20 seconds, then divide the steaks between four plates and spoon over the sauce. Serve with potatoes and vegetables.

Broiled veal kabobs

This recipe originated on the Portuguese island of Madeira, where it is known as *espetada*. It is a great way to tenderize and add flavor to veal. Choose a cut of veal from the loin or leg.

Serves 4

Thread the veal onto four skewers and lay flat in a shallow, nonmetallic dish. Mix together the garlic, bay leaf, herbs, wine, and oil and season with black pepper. Drizzle over the veal, turning to coat, then leave in a cool place for 2 hours, turning occasionally.

Preheat the broiler. Remove the veal from the marinade and pat dry on paper towels. Brush lightly with oil and broil, turning occasionally, until just cooked through. Sprinkle with salt and serve.

1¼–1½ lb veal, cut into
1-inch cubes
1–2 plump garlic
cloves, crushed
1 bay leaf, torn in half
a small handful of parsley
mixed with a little fresh
marjoram, chopped
6 tbsp red or dry white wine
2 tbsp olive oil, plus extra
for brushing

Veal with onion and tuna sauce

This classic Italian dish, known as *vitello tonnato*, makes an elegant summer supper. It is the perfect prepare-ahead meal for relaxed entertaining. Choose a cut from the leg, which is ideal for braising.

Serves 6–8

2¼ lb boneless veal
roast, trimmed
12 anchovy fillets, chopped
3 onions, finely chopped
2 tbsp capers, roughly chopped
6 black peppercorns
4 large parsley sprigs
2 cups (16 fl oz) chicken or
vegetable broth
3½ oz canned tuna, drained
1 shallot, finely chopped
1 tbsp tomato paste
Juice of 1 lemon
1 cup (8 fl oz) mayonnaise
2 tbsp chopped flat-leaf parsley

Put the veal onto a cutting board and butterfly it, slicing it open—without cutting completely through—into one large, evenly thick piece. Pound half the anchovies, one of the chopped onions, the capers, and a little black pepper together into a chunky paste, then rub over the veal. Roll up the veal, tie it securely, then place in a pan just large enough to hold it.

Press the remaining chopped onions, peppercorns, and parsley around the veal, then pour in just enough broth to cover it. Bring to a boil, then half-cover and simmer gently for 2 hours, until the veal is just tender. Let cool in the broth, then chill (ideally overnight).

To make the tuna sauce, purée the tuna in a blender with the shallot, remaining anchovies, tomato paste, lemon juice, and mayonnaise. Season with black pepper and stir in the parsley. Slice the veal, arrange on a plate, and spoon over the sauce.

Spiced oxtails with buckwheat

This recipe, adapted from one popular in the Lower Volga region of Russia, requires long, slow cooking but the meltingly tender results are well worth it.

Serves 6–8

In a large pan, brown the oxtail pieces in the oil. Remove with a slotted spoon and set aside. Add the onion and fry until softened. Stir in the garlic and cook for 1 minute, then stir in the tomato paste, tomatoes, broth, cinnamon, cumin, ginger, mustard seeds, turmeric, parsley, and cilantro. Return the meat to the pan. Bring to a boil, cover, and simmer gently for 4 hours, topping up with water if necessary, until the meat is falling from the bone. Cool, then chill for 12 hours or overnight.

Preheat the oven to 350°F (180°C). Toast the buckwheat in an ovenproof pan over a medium heat until it begins to pop. Add 2½ cups (20 fl oz) boiling water, a pinch of salt, and the butter. Bake in the oven for 45 minutes or until the grains are soft. Meanwhile, discard the solidified fat from the oxtail dish. Remove the oxtail pieces and transfer to a baking dish. Pour over enough boiling water to cover the base of the dish, cover with foil, and reheat in the oven for 30 minutes. Strain the tomato sauce mixture. Tip back into the pan with the carrots, turnips, and celeriac. Bring to a boil, cover, and simmer for 10 minutes. Stir in the zucchini and leeks and cook until the vegetables are tender, about 10 minutes. Strain the oxtail and add the cooking liquid to the vegetable mixture. Bring the sauce to a boil.

Spoon the buckwheat onto a large serving plate with the oxtails and vegetable mixture. Garnish with sprigs of parsley and cilantro.

5 lb oxtail pieces, trimmed
4 tbsp sunflower oil
3 medium onions, sliced
4 garlic cloves, crushed
1½ tbsp tomato paste
1¾ cups (14 fl oz) canned chopped tomatoes with chile
3¾ cups (30 fl oz) beef broth
3 cinnamon sticks
1 tsp ground cumin
1 tsp ground ginger
1 tsp mustard seeds
¾ tsp turmeric
4 tbsp each finely chopped parsley and cilantro, plus extra to garnish
2 cups (12 oz) buckwheat groats (kasha)
2 tbsp butter
3 carrots, halved and thinly sliced
12 oz turnips, halved and thinly sliced
1 small celeriac, quartered and thinly sliced
2 medium zucchini, halved and thinly sliced
½ lb baby leeks, trimmed and left whole

PORK

Pork is the name of the meat taken from the pig animal or carcass. Almost all parts of the animal can be eaten and the meat can be sold fresh, precooked, cured, marinated, or smoked. Pork is generally lean and tender and its flavor goes with various herbs, aromatic seasonings, and fruit, such as apples and peaches. Pork is a versatile meat and can be roasted, broiled, fried, stewed, braised, or poached. Fresh pork should be moist and pink; avoid cuts that are gray or red.

Primal cuts

The primal cuts are those made in the initial stage of butchering. They may be sold whole, or subdivided into smaller cuts for sale to home cooks.

Arm shoulder

Whole shoulder

Loin

Leg

Side

Whole shoulder

The shoulder primal can be divided into two sub-cuts for roasts, braises, and pork chops: the blade shoulder in the upper section and the sparerib chops taken from underneath. Chops cut from the shoulder are tougher than loin chops. The economical blade roast can be bone-in or boneless.

Flavor

The blade shoulder is relatively lean, with great flavor, though it can be quite tough. Rectangular-shaped sparerib chops from the shoulder are particularly succulent and flavorful because of the fat running through them.

Cooking

Blade roast is best suited to roasting or slow cooking in moist heat, such as braising. It can also be cubed for stewing or ground into burgers and sausages. Sparerib pork chops are best suited to braising, broiling, grilling, and barbecuing.

Also known as

Blade pork chops, shoulder butt, upper shoulder or Boston shoulder, chuck. Economical cuts from the blade are also known as grillades *(French)* and are used in the Louisiana dish grillades and grits.

Substitutes

Loin roast or loin chop.

Arm shoulder

The arm shoulder primal is taken from beneath the blade shoulder and includes the top of the foreleg. It can be cut into roasts or steaks for braising or stewing. It is ideal for using in sausages and in processed food.

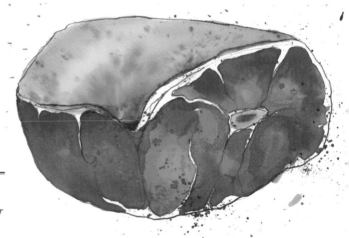

Flavor

The arm shoulder is a tougher cut than the blade shoulder. It is lean and therefore not particularly flavorful.

Cooking

Roasts or steaks can be braised or stewed. Cuts from the arm shoulder can also be ground down for burgers.

Also known as

Hand of pork.

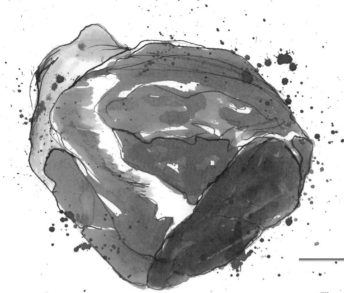

Flavor

The picnic shoulder is
moderately flavorful. It can be
smoked for extra flavor.

Picnic shoulder

The picnic shoulder is cut from the arm shoulder primal at the thick end of the belly (side). It can be either bone-in or boned and can be cut into steaks. The arm picnic roast contains the arm, shank, and cushion. If the shank is removed it is known as pork shoulder arm roast. It can be subdivided into a smaller cut called the picnic cushion and into arm steaks.

Cooking

Roasts are best suited to
roasting or slow cooking in
moist heat, such as braising.
The picnic shoulder can be
roasted, braised, or poached.
It can be barbecued and is
delicious as pulled pork. It
is sliced and eaten cold for
picnics. Steaks are best suited
to grilling, frying, or braising.

Also known as

Arm picnic roast.

Hock

Hock is the lower portion of the foreleg, beneath the shank. It is an economical cut containing the shank bone and the skin. Hock contains a lot of connective tissue and is relatively tough unless cooked slowly.

Flavor

It is naturally flavorful but often smoked for extra flavor.

Cooking

Hock is best cooked slowly in moist heat, such as braising or stewing, to break down the connective tissue. It gives out a thick jelly when cooked and is therefore used to add richness and flavor to stocks, stews, and braises.

Also known as

Knuckle of bacon (when smoked).

Loin

The loin primal consists of the pig animal's back between the shoulder and the hind leg. The loin can be cut into roasts and chops.

Canadian-style bacon is cut from the loin. The chump end is a continuation of the loin; it runs toward the hind leg and can be cut into roasts or steaks.

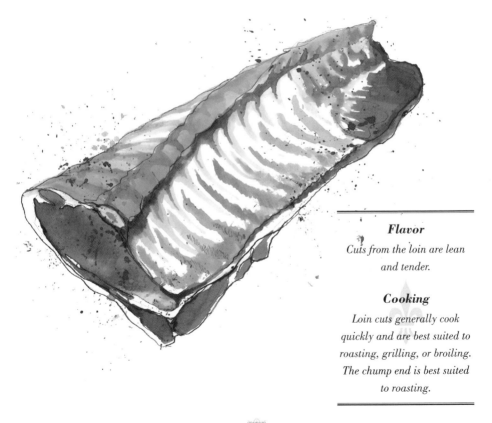

Flavor
Cuts from the loin are lean and tender.

Cooking
Loin cuts generally cook quickly and are best suited to roasting, grilling, or broiling. The chump end is best suited to roasting.

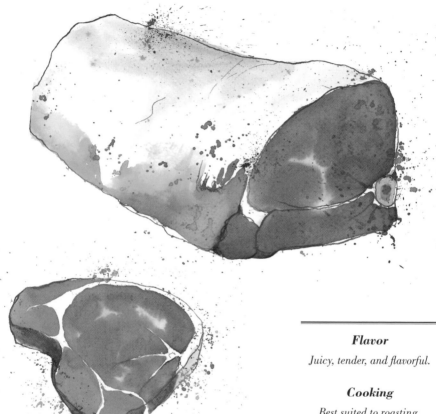

Flavor

Juicy, tender, and flavorful.

Cooking

Best suited to roasting, grilling, and broiling.

Hind loin

This is a more expensive cut from the center of the loin. It consists of the tenderloin, loin eye, and T-bones and makes an impressive roast to serve at the table. It can also be cut into pork chops.

Also known as

Center loin and sirloin end roast.

Flavor

Tender, juicy, and flavorful.

Cooking

Loin roasts are best suited to roasting, grilling, and broiling. Chops are best suited to grilling, broiling, or frying. Cutlets can be fried, broiled, or sliced into strips and stir-fried.

Also known as

Rib loin, rack of pork, sirloin roast (bone-in), and carré de porc *(French). Two racks of ribs curved and tied together is known as a crown roast.*

Fore loin

The fore loin is cut from the rib end of the loin and consists of the rib bones, hip bone, backbone, and loin eye muscle; it can include the larger end of the tenderloin. It can be cut into chops or cutlets. It can be bone-in or boned and rolled. If the chine bone (backbone) has been removed, it is known as having been chined. If the fat has been removed to expose the rib bones, it is described as Frenched.

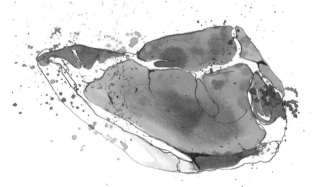

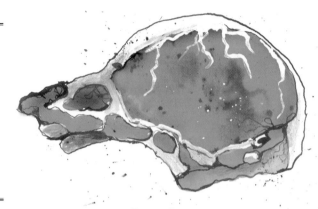

Flavor

Loin chops are the most tender of all pork chops with good flavor.

Cooking

They are best suited to grilling, broiling, frying, or braising.

Loin chops

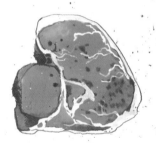

Loin chops cut from the fore loin are a relatively expensive choice. They contain the T-bone and a section of the loin and tenderloin. Traditionally the chop included a slice of the kidney, though this is now rare. They can be bone-in or boneless depending on whether the chine bone has been removed. Boneless loin chops can be butterflied open by being sliced almost in half and flattened out.

Top loin roast

The top loin roast is a boneless cut and contains the loin eye muscle. Two top loin roasts can be tied together, fat side out, to become a loin double roast.

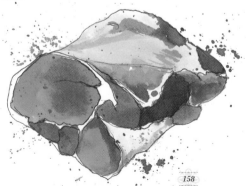

Flavor

Tender, succulent, and flavorful.

Cooking

Best suited to roasting, broiling, or grilling.

Also known as

Boneless loin of pork.

Ribs

Pork ribs, cut from the rib section within the loin, consist of the bones and meat between them. They are best suited to slow, moist cooking, such as braising, but can also be grilled or broiled.

Country-style ribs

Cut from the fore or rib end of the loin, these popular ribs are small and meaty. They come in slabs of 8 to 14 ribs and can be a relatively pricy choice. They are shorter and meatier than spareribs from the belly and take well to being marinated or seasoned by a rub before being braised. Also known as loin ribs, back ribs, and baby-back ribs.

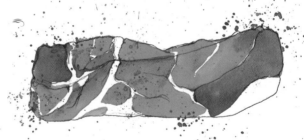

Flat bone riblets

These are small and flat in shape. Also known as button ribs.

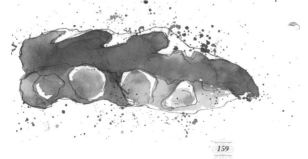

Tenderloin

This is a long, boneless, wedge-shaped piece from the loin that runs alongside the backbone. The thin end toward the fore loin can be cut into smaller pieces called tenderloin tips.

Flavor

The tenderloin is incredibly tender. It is not particularly flavorful because it is so lean.

Cooking

Best suited to fast cooking, such as roasting, grilling, or broiling. Take care not to overcook tenderloin because it can dry out easily. For this reason it is often stuffed and rolled to retain its succulence. It responds well to marinating to increase its flavor and is often served with cream sauces. Tenderloin tips can be fried or stir-fried.

Also known as

Pork fillet.

Side

The side primal is cut from the underside of the pig carcass between the fore and hind legs. It consists of the pork belly and spareribs. Pork brisket bones and rib tips can also be cut from the side. Cuts from the side can be cured and turned into bacon.

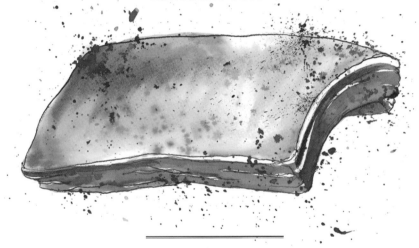

Flavor

The side has a good flavor due to its high fat content.

Cooking

Cuts from the side are best suited to slow roasting, braising, and stewing. Bacon can be broiled, grilled, or fried.

Pork belly

Pork belly is fatty, tough, and relatively cheap. It can be sold boned, stuffed, or rolled.

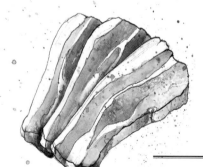

Flavor

Pork belly has an extremely good flavor due to its high ratio of fat to meat.

Cooking

Pork belly is suitable for a variety of moist cooking methods, including slow-roasting, braising, stewing, and barbecuing. Pieces can be cut into strips and grilled or broiled. Pork belly responds well to marinating—particularly using Asian flavors—and can also be prepared as a confit, a terrine, or shredded into rillettes.

Also known as

Pork side or trimmed belly.

Spareribs

Spareribs are cut out in one piece from the inside of the belly on the underside of the pig carcass. They can be quite meaty but contain a certain amount of fat and connective tissue. Spareribs are long and make great finger food at parties and barbecues. They contain at least 11 bones.

Flavor

The fattiness of this cut makes it ideal for barbecuing, and the meaty flavor can take on strong marinades and sauces, such as a sweet and sour sauce.

Cooking

Spareribs are best suited to roasting, braising, or barbecuing, and because of the high quantity of connective tissue, they are also well suited to slow cooking in moist heat.

Also known as

Barbecue ribs, American pork ribs, and enterro *(Mexico). When spareribs are trimmed into a square shape they are known as St. Louis-style ribs. If the front bone is removed they are known as Kansas City-style. Riblets are spareribs that have been cut in half to produce short ribs; they are an economical cut designed to stretch farther.*

Leg

The leg primal is the hind leg of the pig animal or carcass. It is a great cut for feeding a crowd and can be prepared as a roast, leg cutlets, or steaks. It can also be cured and smoked on the bone into ham.

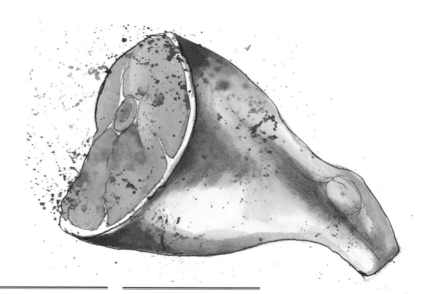

Flavor

Cuts from the leg are fairly lean and flavorful, though sometimes tough. The most tender cuts come from higher up the leg, farthest from the ground.

Cooking

Leg can be cut into roasts and steaks for braising, slow roasting, poaching, frying, or broiling. For roasting, choose a leg roast that has a good covering of fat.

Top and bottom leg roasts and steaks

These are boneless, economical roasts and steaks. They are cut from just above the knee and are a good-value choice.

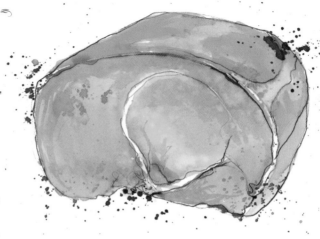

Flavor

Roasts have a good flavor though leg steaks can sometimes be a little tough because they are relatively lean. Their flavor is dependent on the amount of fat they contain and the quality of the animal they come from.

Cooking

Roasts are suitable for roasting. The steaks are best marinated to tenderize the meat before braising, frying, grilling, or broiling. They can also be cut into strips for stir-fries.

Also known as

Tip roast and tri-tip steaks.

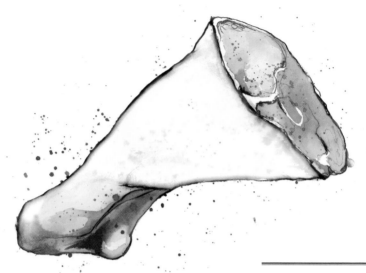

Flavor

Excellent flavor when cooked correctly.

Shank

Cooking

Shank becomes meltingly tender when cooked slowly in liquid, such as braising or poaching.

The shank is the cut below the knee of the hind leg. It contains the leg bone, which is rich in gelatin and can be used to add lots of flavor and richness to stocks and stews. Shank can be cooked whole, or sliced into cross-cut steaks containing the shank bone.

Also known as

Hind shank and knuckle.

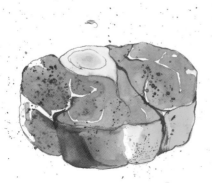

Inside and outside rounds

These are boneless cuts taken from the inside and outside of the leg.
The outside round is a little tougher and is therefore a cheaper cut.

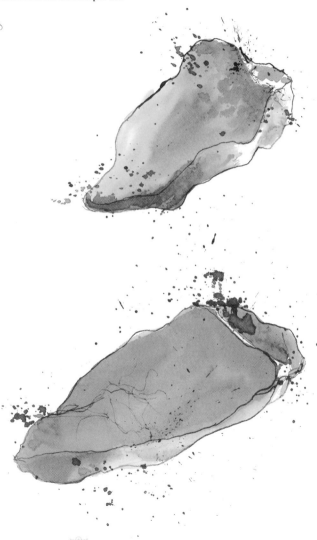

Flavor

Both rounds can be relatively
tender when cooked correctly.

Cooking

The inside round is best suited
to roasting or can be cut up for
stews and soups. The outside
round can be relatively tough
and is best suited to slow-
roasting or braising.

Also known as

Boneless pork leg.

Variety meats

Variety meats are cuts taken from the extremities of the animal or the organs within. They are also known as offal or innards.

Neck bones

The small bones from the neck of the pig are meaty and cheap to buy. The meat is rich and chewy and is sometimes smoked. When simmered in soups, smoked neck bones can be an economical alternative to smoked ham. They can be also be poached or braised to add flavor to green vegetables, stocks, and stews. They are also known as collar bones (British) and *collo* (Italian).

Pigs' feet

Pigs' feet are taken from the bottom of the fore and hind legs of the pig and sometimes include part of the shank. Pigs' feet contain little meat and are best used in stocks to add a rich, gelatinous flavor and texture. They are suited to long, slow cooking in liquid, such as braising, and can be pickled after cooking and eaten as a snack. They are also known as trotters (British), *pata* (Spanish), and crubeens (when cooked).

Kidneys

Like cows' kidneys, pigs' kidneys can be relatively tough and are best suited to long, slow cooking in moist heat. To prepare them, remove the outer membrane, cut the kidneys in half, and discard the white fat in the middle. If you find the odor or flavor of pigs' kidneys too strong, soak them for an hour in milk or water with a squeeze of lemon before cooking.

Liver

Pigs' liver is strong-tasting and less desirable in cooking than lambs' or calves' liver. It is best soaked in milk before being slowly cooked in liquid, by braising, poaching, or stewing. Pigs' liver is often finely chopped and used in forcemeats, pâtés, sausages, and terrines.

Tongue

Pork tongue should be light pink
in color. It is tough and so is
best suited to long, slow cooking
in liquid, such as braising,
poaching, or stewing. Tongue is
usually sold precooked and sliced
for sandwiches and salads.

Chitterlings

Chitterlings are the pig's large
intestines. To prepare, rinse
and clean them thoroughly, then
poach or stew with fragrant herbs
for up to six hours. After cooking,
the tenderized chitterlings can
be battered or floured and fried.
Chitterlings can also be chopped
up and used in sausages, for
example in France's *andouillette*.

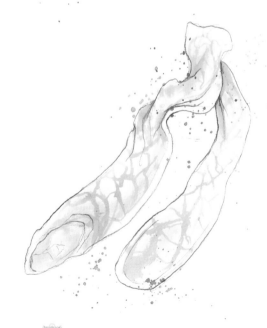

Pork casings

Pork casings are the small
intestines of the pig. They are
traditionally used to encase
sausages, although nowadays
sausage skins are often synthetic.

Heart

Fresh pig's heart should be bright
red and firm, and cheap to buy.
To prepare, rinse in cold water,
then remove any blood vessels or
clots. Pig's heart is best suited to
long, slow cooking in liquid, such
as stewing, poaching, or braising,
and is often chopped up and used
in ragoûts or stews.

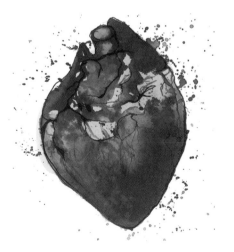

Pig's head

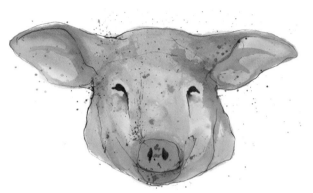

Pig's head can be stewed or braised and the meat used in terrines and pâtés. The cooked meat can also be made into brawn—sometimes known as headcheese—by being seasoned and set in a bowl with the jelly-like aspic from the cooking liquid. Brawn can be sliced for sandwiches and salads. Pig's head is also known as *tête de cochon* (French).

Cheeks

Pigs' cheeks, taken from either side of the head, can be sold as part of the head or separately. They are often cured in brine before being poached or braised until tender and can be eaten hot or cold. They are also known as chaps and *joue* (French).

Jowl

Jowl is a fatty cut taken from the face of the pig and includes all or part of the cheeks. It is often cut up and used to add flavor to stews. When jowl is cured it becomes tender and incredibly flavorful, and is considered a delicacy, particularly in Italy, where it is known as *guanciale*.

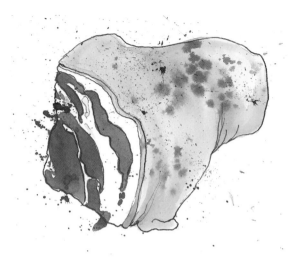

Pigs' ears, snout, and tail

Pigs' ears, snout, and tail are most commonly used in commercial pork meat products, such as sausages, pork pies, and cold meats. They can also be boiled or stewed whole to add flavor and gelatin to stocks. Ears can be roasted and eaten as a snack or sliced into spicy Asian dishes.

Pork fat

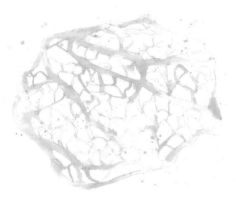

Caul

Caul is a net of fat taken from the pig's stomach. It is wrapped around roasts to baste them as they cook. Before using, soak caul in warm water, then carefully tease it out and pat it dry. Caul is popular in Asian and Mediterranean cooking. It is also known as caul fat.

Fatback

Fatback is the length of firm fat taken from the upper portion of the back and shoulder of the pig, along the top of the loin primal. Sometimes fatback is still attached to the cuts it runs alongside. Alternatively, it can be removed before the loin is broken down and cut into thin sheets that are used to baste roasts. Fatback can be rendered down into lard or chopped into small studs and inserted into lean roasts to help baste them as they cook; this practice is known as larding. Fatback is also cut into small cubes and used in blood sausages (black pudding) and salami. It is also known as back fat.

Lard

Lard can be taken from any fatty tissue of the pig.
Lard taken from around the kidneys is known as
leaf lard and is used in pastries, cookies, cakes, and
for deep-frying. It is available fresh or processed;
processed lard will last longer than fresh. Lard is also
known as *lardo* (Italian) and *panne* (French).

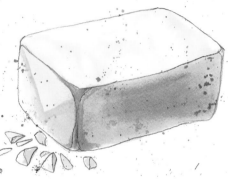

Salt pork

Salt pork is fat taken from the belly and sides of the
pig that has been cured with salt. It contains narrow
streaks of meat and resembles very fatty bacon. Salt
pork is often sold in vacuum packs and can be added
to soups and stews for flavor and richness. For a
milder flavor, soak it in water before using. It is also
known as *petit salé* (French) and *salume* (Italian).

Cured pork

Pork was traditionally cured to preserve it. It can be made into sausages, bacon, ham, and cold cuts for slicing. Cured sausage, such as German or Italian salami, Spanish chorizo, and French saucisson does not need to be cooked and can be eaten cold. Precooked smoked sausages, such as frankfurters, are popular in Germany and cheaper versions are used in hotdogs.

Streaky bacon

Streaky bacon is cut from the belly of the pig. It contains more fat than back bacon, and the streaked effect is caused by the meat and fat running parallel to each other. It can be cooked as whole slices or chopped up and fried with onions to add flavor to soups and stews.

Bacon

Bacon can be cut from the back (loin), side, or belly of the pig. It is either dry-cured in salt and sugar or wet-cured in brine, sometimes with the addition of flavorings, such as honey or spices. Sometimes the brine solution can be injected directly into the meat to speed up the curing process; this results in a less flavorsome bacon that is more prone to shrinking when cooked, as the liquid leaches out. Bacon can be smoked after curing.

Bacon is sold in thin slices as rashers, slices, or strips. The fat and skin—known as the rind—are attached to the slice. Fresh bacon should be firm and damp to the touch without being slimy and should have no odor. Avoid bacon that is streaked with silver or green; it is well past its best. Bacon is best grilled, broiled, or fried and is traditionally eaten for breakfast with eggs in Great Britain and Ireland. Precooked bacon bits can also be used as toppings for pizzas and salads.

Back bacon

Back bacon is cut from the back (loin) of the pig. It is relatively lean, meaty, and firmly textured and can be thickly sliced into bacon steaks for grilling, broiling, frying, or roasting.

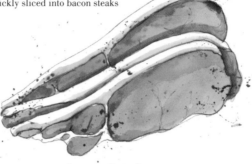

Lardons

Lardons are small cubes of thickly cut bacon, usually taken from the belly of the pig. They can be fried, often with sliced onions, to flavor soups, stews, quiches, and risottos. They can also be fried until crisp and sprinkled over salads to give flavor and texture.

Pancetta

Pancetta is Italian air-dried bacon cut from belly of pork. It can be smoked and sold either as one whole piece or cut into thin slices or cubes for frying. Pancetta has a concentrated flavor and endless culinary uses: it can be chopped into soups, stews, and pasta dishes; whole slices can be wrapped around chicken and fish before roasting; or it can be fried until crisp and sprinkled over salads.

Prosciutto

Prosciutto is the Italian word for ham and it can be either *crudo* (raw) or *cotto* (cooked). The ham is preserved by curing and air-drying for up to two years before being cut into wafer-thin slices and served as an antipasto or in salads. Prosciutto can be made all over Italy but prosciutto di Parma is the best-known (see right).

Parma ham

True Parma ham must come from a certain breed of pig in Parma, Italy. The ham is cured with a mix of dry and wet salt. This is a slow process and its production is subject to strict monitoring and controls. The meat is delicate and flavorsome and is usually eaten cold as part of antipasto. If Parma ham is left on the bone it will continue to mature and develop in flavor.

Salami

Salami is a firm sausage made from finely chopped fat and meat—often pork—plus seasonings, such as garlic, peppercorns, and herbs. It is usually cured or brined and sometimes smoked. Salami can be sliced and eaten cold or cooked into stews and sauces. Pepperoni is an American take on salami, often used on pizza toppings or in sandwiches.

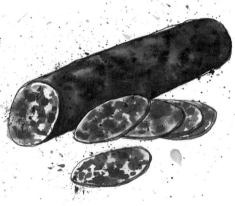

Chorizo

Chorizo is a spiced sausage, popular in Spain and Portugal (where it is known as *chouriço*). It is made from chopped meat—pork or beef—and fat, and is seasoned with a variety of ingredients, including smoked paprika, which provides its distinctive red color and smoky flavor. Chorizo is air-dried and sometimes smoked. It can range from mild to spicy in flavor and can be sliced and eaten cold, tapas-style, or cooked into stews and sauces.

Techniques

Scoring fat on a pork roast

Scoring the top fat on a roast of pork before roasting will produce delicious, crispy crackling and helps the fat to baste and tenderize the meat as it cooks.

First, make sure the rind is completely dry; pat it dry with paper towel if it is damp or wet.

Using a sharp knife, score through the rind evenly at ¼-inch intervals in a criss-cross pattern.

Rub salt and olive oil into the slashes. You may wish to flavor the roast further by rubbing in extra ingredients, such as minced garlic, grated lemon zest, or chopped herbs.

Weigh the pork, put it onto a trivet in a roasting pan, and roast according to the calculated cooking time until the crackling is crisp and golden and the meat is cooked through. Remove the crackling before carving the meat, and snap it into pieces.

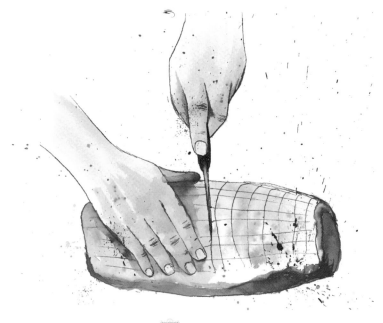

Preparing and cooking pork medallions

Medallions are round slices of boneless meat that are tender enough to be fried, broiled, or grilled. Pork medallions can be cut from the tenderloin; one tenderloin will serve two to three people.

Remove the silver membrane that runs along the top of the tenderloin.

Cut the tenderloin into 1-inch-thick slices. Cover the slices with wet plastic wrap or nonstick parchment paper and bat out with a meat tenderizer. Season with salt and pepper.

Heat a little oil in a large skillet and fry the medallions for 2 to 3 minutes on each side until golden and cooked through—do this in batches if necessary. Remove the medallions from the pan to make a pan sauce (see page 182), then return to the pan to heat through just before serving.

Making a pan sauce for pork

Using the cooking juices to make a rich, flavorsome sauce will add lots of extra flavor to the finished dish and can easily be done while the meat is resting.

When the meat is cooked, remove it from the pan, cover with foil, and let rest in a warm place. Drain away any excess fat from the pan, then add a splash of wine, stock, or cider. Put the pan over a low heat and use a spatula to scrape up any browned, caramelized pieces stuck to the bottom; this is where all the flavor is.

Gradually add a good-quality, hot stock, stirring constantly, until the liquid is bubbling. You may wish to flavor it further with additional ingredients, such as mushrooms, chopped onions, herbs, or mustard. Once the liquid is starting to thicken, add a splash of cream. Return the meat to the pan to warm through with the sauce or serve the sauce poured over the meat.

Cooking pigs' feet

Remove any hair from the feet—the easiest way to do this is to singe the hairs off. Soak the feet in cold water in the refrigerator for 24 hours. Remove from the water and put them into a large deep-sided pan with chopped vegetables, such as carrot, onion, and celery. Add a bouquet garni and enough cold water to cover the feet. Bring to a boil and simmer for 3 to 4 hours, topping up with water as necessary, until the feet are tender. Cool in the liquid, then remove with a slotted spoon. They should split in half quite easily. The cooked feet may then be floured and fried or broiled for extra flavor.

Preparing a suckling pig for roasting

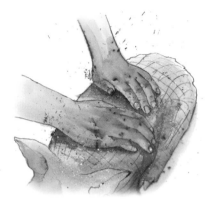

Suckling pigs are unweaned piglets that have been slaughtered at between two and four weeks of age. The meat is pale and tender and is served with the golden, crisp crackling skin. Allow one suckling pig to serve around 10 people.

To prepare, slash through the skin and fat all over the pig, except the head. Make a herb rub by mixing salt, chopped fresh herbs, grated lemon zest, and black pepper. Rub into the cavity of the pig and into the slashes, then keep in a cool place for up to 24 hours to allow the flavors to develop.

Preheat the oven to 400°F (200°C). Weigh the pig and calculate the cooking time at 15 minutes per pound. Put the pig, belly-side down, onto a wire rack in a large roasting pan (the rack will allow the hot air to circulate freely and help the meat to cook evenly). Cover the snout and ears with foil to keep them from burning and brush the pig all over with oil. Roast for 20 to 30 minutes, then lower the temperature to 350°F (180°C) and roast for the calculated cooking time, basting regularly with the juices, until golden on the outside and cooked through. Suckling pig can be served hot or cold. It is also known as *cochon de lait* (French) and piglet.

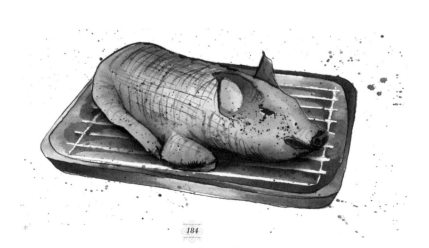

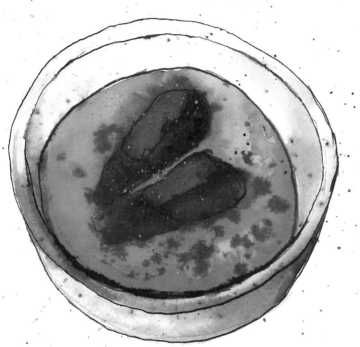

Marinating ribs for the barbecue

To make a tasty marinade for ribs, put some grated gingerroot, minced garlic, honey, lemon juice, hoisin sauce, and chopped herbs in a pan. Heat gently, stirring, to dissolve the honey. Let cool, then rub the marinade into the ribs. Let marinate in the refrigerator for at least 1 hour in a nonmetallic dish or a resealable plastic bag. The thinner the marinade, the faster it will penetrate the meat; the thinner the ribs, the faster the marinade will take hold. Baste the ribs with your favorite barbecue sauce as they cook, for extra flavor.

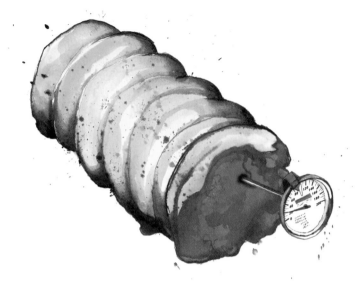

Testing pork for doneness

A meat thermometer is an inexpensive investment for accurately testing the doneness of meat. A meat thermometer may be placed in the thickest part of the raw meat before cooking, so you can check the temperature without opening the oven door. Alternatively, it can be inserted into the roast just before the calculated cooking time is up. Transfer the roast to a board and push a meat thermometer into its thickest part; hold for 15 seconds. Pork should be cooked until well-done, with a minimum core temperature of 170°F (75°C), but remove it from the oven just before it reaches this, because the meat will carry on cooking as it rests.

Carving a bone-in loin of pork

Remove the roast from the oven and put it onto a warmed plate. Cover it with foil and rest it in a warm place for up to 30 minutes.

Transfer the roast to a carving board. Using a sharp carving knife, cut carefully between the meat and the crackling. Remove the crackling and cut it into small pieces along the scored marks.

Cut along the length of the roast to remove the backbone. Sit the roast on this flattened edge, then carve between the rib bones to separate them into pieces. For smaller slices, slice more thinly so that every other piece contains a rib bone. Alternatively, tease the meat from the bones, then slice it off, leaving the bones in place. Arrange the slices on a warmed serving platter with the crackling.

Pork and lentil stew

This is a robust one-pot dish that uses a shoulder cut of pork and is incredibly simple to prepare.

Serves 6

*2 cups (1 lb) green or
brown lentils
2 onions, chopped
1 carrot, chopped
4 garlic cloves, halved
lengthwise
1 red bell pepper, seeded
and chopped
½ lb blood sausage
½ lb chorizo
½ lb fresh picnic shoulder, cut
into chunks
1 bay leaf, torn in half
A few parsley sprigs
2 tbsp olive oil*

Put all the ingredients into a Dutch oven. Add enough water to cover by about 1 inch, then bring to a boil. Simmer gently for 30 to 40 minutes, topping up with water when necessary, until the meat and lentils are tender and the liquid has almost evaporated.

Remove the blood sausage and chorizo. Slice, and return to the stew. Mix well, then serve with rice or potatoes.

Stir-fried ground pork

This speedy dish is a great way to add lots of flavor to ground pork. Serve with noodles or rice.

Serves 4–6

Put all the ingredients for the marinade into a small pan and heat gently for 5 minutes, stirring. Cool, then mix into the ground pork. Set aside to marinate.

Heat the oil in a large skillet or wok. Add the garlic, fry for 1 minute, then add the marinated pork. Fry over a high heat for 3 minutes, stirring constantly, then add the olives, mushrooms, and chile. Stir-fry for 3 minutes or until the pork is cooked.

9 oz ground pork
1 tbsp peanut oil
1 tsp minced garlic
1 tbsp black olives,
  finely chopped
½ lb button mushrooms, sliced
1 red chile pepper, finely sliced

For the marinade:

1 tsp cornstarch
2 tsp light soy sauce
1 tsp sugar
1 tsp rice wine
2 tbsp peanut oil

Roast pork with apple–walnut stuffing

This is a simple yet elegant dish using pork loin. The crunch of walnuts, the touch of spice, and the sweetness of the golden raisins go perfectly with the succulent meat.

Serves 8

6 tbsp butter, chopped

2 large, tart apples, peeled, cored, and cut into ½-inch chunks

1 small onion, chopped

2 celery stalks, chopped

1 garlic clove, finely chopped

3 cups (6 oz) soft bread crumbs

1 cup (4 oz) walnut pieces

½ cup (3 oz) golden raisins

¼ tsp ground cloves

½ tsp powdered mustard

1 boneless pork loin roast, weighing about 3 lb

3 tbsp vegetable oil

To make the stuffing, melt 3 tbsp butter in a medium skillet. Add the apples and fry for 8 to 10 minutes until soft. Tip into a large bowl and set aside. Add the remaining butter to the pan and fry the onion, celery, and garlic for 5 minutes until softened. Add to the apples with the bread crumbs, walnuts, golden raisins, cloves, and mustard. Season with salt and mix well. If the mixture is very firm add a splash of milk to loosen it. Set aside.

Preheat the oven to 375°F (190°C).

Cut the pork almost in half lengthwise. Flatten it out and make slashes lengthwise along its thickest parts. Spoon the stuffing over the pork, pressing into each slash. Carefully bring up the sides of the roast and tightly tie into a roll. Push any stuffing back into the roast as you tie it.

Heat the oil in a large skillet. Add the pork and sauté quickly until golden all over. Transfer the meat to a board, placing it on top of four lengths of kitchen string.

Weigh the stuffed roast and calculate the cooking time at 25 minutes per pound. Put the stuffed roast onto a trivet in a roasting pan and roast according to the calculated cooking time or until cooked through. Let the pork rest for 15 minutes before carving.

Pork with cabbage and corn

This is a hearty one-pot pork rib dish that's full of flavor. If you can't get hold of fresh corn, frozen is fine.

Serves 6

Put the pork ribs into a Dutch oven. Add just enough water to cover, then cook on the stovetop over medium heat for 1 to 1½ hours or until the meat is tender. Add the onion and tomatoes and cook for a further 10 minutes.

Blend the garlic, cumin, peppercorns, and vinegar in a food processor. Add to the pork mixture with the cabbage and corn. Stir well and season. Cook for 5 minutes or until the cabbage is just tender. Serve with rice.

1½ lb pork loin ribs, chopped
1 medium onion, sliced
2 large tomatoes, sliced
2 garlic cloves
A pinch of cumin seeds
8 peppercorns
2 tbsp vinegar
1 medium cabbage, sliced
1½ cups (12 oz) corn kernels

Spiced pork and eggplant chop suey

This spiced Chinese-style dish of marinated pork tenderloin and crisp vegetables is delicious served with rice or noodles.

Serves 4

1 pork tenderloin, weighing about 1 lb, trimmed and thinly sliced
1½ lb mixed stir-fry vegetables, such as carrots, bell peppers, snow peas, and bean sprouts
1 eggplant, halved lengthwise and sliced thinly
4 tbsp peanut oil

For the marinade:

2-inch piece gingerroot, roughly grated
2 garlic cloves, crushed
1 tbsp five-spice powder
1 fresh green chile pepper, seeded and finely chopped
4 tbsp soy sauce
1 tbsp chili sauce
1 tbsp light brown sugar

To make the marinade, squeeze the juice from the grated gingerroot and mix with the remaining marinade ingredients. Add the pork and toss to coat in the mixture. Marinate for 1 hour, turning occasionally.

Meanwhile, cut the vegetables into 2-inch lengths. Heat the oil in a wok or large skillet until almost smoking, then add the marinated pork with the eggplant. Stir-fry for 4 to 5 minutes until golden, then add the remaining vegetables and any remaining marinade. Cook until liquid is very hot and simmering, then serve immediately with rice or noodles.

Tolosa red bean stew with pork

This pork belly dish is from Tolosa in the Spanish Basque country, a region famous for its love of red beans and highly seasoned sausages like chorizo.

Serves 4

Drain the beans and put them in a pot with the pork and half the chopped onion. Add 1 tablespoon of oil and cover with water. Bring to a boil, turn down the heat, cover, and simmer gently for 2 hours or until the meat is almost tender. Check regularly that the water level remains high enough, adding more if necessary to stop the stew from drying out.

Fry the ham fat to give off grease, or heat the oil in a pan. Slice the chorizos and fry them with the chopped bell pepper.

Remove the pork or bacon from the beans and chop it into cubes. Check the amount of liquid in the pot: it should now be well reduced (if not, pour some off). Add all the meats to the pot and season everything well.

Fry the remaining onion in the same pan you used for the sausage, adding the garlic at the end. Stir into the beans and simmer 10 minutes more, then serve.

1 lb red beans, soaked
overnight
5 oz pork belly or boiling
bacon, in one piece
1 large onion, finely chopped
2 tbsp olive oil
2 tbsp chopped ham fat or
more olive oil
2 chorizo sausages
1 large green bell pepper,
seeded and chopped
Salt and freshly ground
black pepper
2 garlic cloves, finely chopped

Roasted spareribs with lemongrass and chile

This is a simple and tasty Asian-style way to add flavor to spareribs.

Serves 4–6

Wash and dry the spareribs and put them in a large bowl.

12 pork spareribs

2 tbsp clear honey

1 tsp five-spice powder

2 cloves garlic, minced

3 tbsp dry sherry or rice wine

3 tbsp fish sauce or 3 tbsp light

soy sauce mixed with 1 tsp

anchovy essence

2 stalks fresh lemongrass,

thinly sliced

2 fresh red chiles, finely

chopped

In another bowl, combine the honey, five-spice powder, garlic, dry sherry, fish sauce, lemon grass, and chile. Mix well. Spread the honey mixture over the spareribs and leave to marinate for 4 hours.

The ribs can be grilled on a barbecue, turning frequently and basting with the marinade; baked in an oven preheated to 325°F (170°C); or broiled under a moderately hot broiler, again, basting regularly with the marinade.

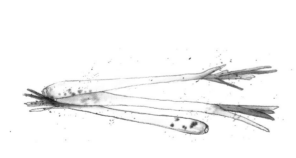

Roast pork Puerto Rican-style

This is a great way of cooking a leg of pork. It's a favorite dish in Puerto Rico where it is loved for its fresh, spicy flavors.

Serves 8–10

Fry the garlic in the olive oil for 1 minute. Tip into a food processor and blend to a paste with the oregano, cumin, scallions, cilantro, bell pepper, and rum. Season with salt and pepper.

Put the leg of pork into a roasting pan. Score the top of the roast into a diamond pattern, cutting through the rind and fat. Rub the garlic paste into the slashes, cover, and let marinate overnight in the refrigerator.

Preheat the oven to 325°F (170°C).

Unwrap the pork and roast in the oven for 2 hours. Add the potatoes, onions, and squash to the roasting pan and baste with the fat. Roast for 1 hour, then add the zucchini and baste with the fat. Roast for a further 45 minutes until the meat is cooked through and the vegetables are tender. Transfer the meat to a carving board, cover loosely with foil, and let rest for 15 minutes. Arrange the vegetables in a serving dish and keep warm.

To make the gravy, pour the excess fat from the roasting pan into a container and discard. Sprinkle the flour over the drippings in the roasting pan and stir over medium heat until smooth, scraping up any browned bits from the bottom of the pan. Gradually beat in the beef broth or water until blended. Bring to a boil, reduce the heat, and simmer for 5 minutes or until thickened, stirring occasionally. Slice the pork and serve with the vegetables and gravy.

1 tbsp minced garlic
3 tbsp olive oil
½ tsp dried oregano
leaves, finely crumbled
¾ tsp ground cumin
4 large scallions, chopped
1 large bunch
cilantro, chopped
1 green bell pepper, seeded
and chopped
1 cup (8 fl oz) white rum
1 leg of pork, weighing about
7 lb with bone
2 large baking potatoes,
scrubbed and cut into wedges
2 large red onions, cut
into wedges
½ butternut squash, peeled
and cut into 1-inch slices
3 zucchini, cut into
1-inch slices

For the gravy:

4 tbsp fat from dripping in
roasting pan
¼ cup (1 oz) flour
3¾ cups (30 fl oz) beef broth
or water

Explosive-fried kidney with cilantro

Explosive-frying involves cooking with very intense heat and is particularly suitable for ingredients with a delicate texture.

Serves 4

4 pigs' kidneys
2 pieces pork stomach
2 tbsp cornstarch
2 tbsp peanut oil
1 tsp chopped garlic
1 large bunch cilantro stalks,
cut into 1½-inch lengths
8 tbsp hot chicken stock
1 tbsp soy sauce
1 tsp Chinese rice wine
1 tsp toasted sesame oil

Split the kidneys in half, remove the fat, membrane, and gristle, and rub with 1 tbsp salt. Wash them thoroughly and soak for 30 minutes.

Split the stomach and rub all over with 1 tbsp salt. Wash and rub it with the cornstarch until it is completely clean. Score into a diamond pattern and cut it into slices. Drain the kidneys and cut into slices.

Heat the oil in a large pan and add the garlic, kidneys, and stomach, stirring over a very high heat for 30 seconds. Add the cilantro stalks and chicken stock and bring to a boil. Drain off the stock and add the soy sauce, rice wine, and toasted sesame oil, stir-frying over a very high heat for 20 seconds. Serve immediately.

Pigs' feet stew

This simple Vietnamese dish is packed with flavor and requires little preparation.

Serves 4

2 lb pigs' feet (trotters),
washed, blanched, and
chopped into 2-inch pieces
5 cups (40 fl oz) chicken or
pork stock
1 large onion, sliced
3 boiled potatoes, quartered
3 tomatoes, diced
2 oz green beans, sliced
1 cup (4 oz) bean sprouts
3 tbsp chopped scallions,
to garnish

Wrap the ingredients for the bouquet garni in a square of cheesecloth and tie into a bundle with string.

Put the feet into a large pan. Cover with water, bring to a boil, and simmer for 2 to 3 hours or until the meat comes away from the bone. Drain, then tip back into the pan with the stock and enough water to cover the feet. Bring to a boil, add the bouquet garni to the pot, and simmer for 10 minutes or until the liquid is slightly thickened.

Add the onion, potatoes, and tomatoes and simmer for 5 minutes. Add the beans and cook for 2 minutes, until tender. Add the bean sprouts and remove the bouquet garni. Sprinkle with the extra cilantro and chopped scallions, then serve immediately.

For the Vietnamese bouquet garni:

2 large celery stalks with
leaves, roughly chopped
3 large bunches cilantro,
including stalks, plus
extra to garnish
2 large lemon grass
stalks, chopped
6 large garlic cloves,
finely chopped
1 cinnamon stick
2 star anise
1 tbsp black peppercorns

LAMB

Lamb is the meat taken from a young sheep that has been slaughtered in the first year of its life. Because the animal is young when slaughtered, most cuts are relatively tender and delicate. The texture and flavor of lamb responds well to marinating, and cuts can be roasted, fried, broiled, grilled, or slow-cooked in moist heat. Meat from a sheep over one year old is known as mutton; hogget refers to the meat taken from a sheep over two years old.

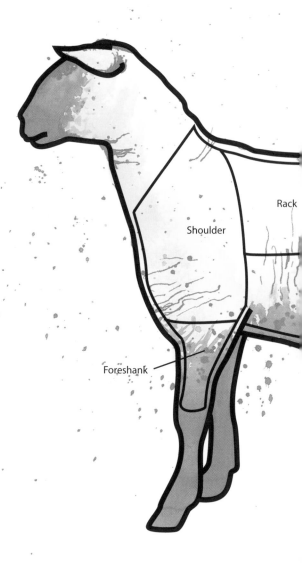

Rack

Shoulder

Foreshank

Primal cuts

The primal cuts are those made in the initial stage of butchering. They may be sold whole, or subdivided into smaller cuts for sale to home cooks.

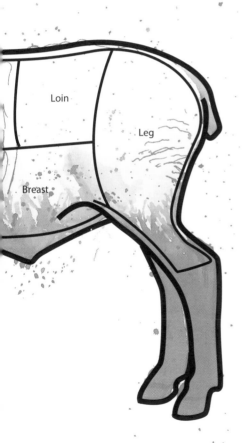

Loin

Leg

Breast

Shoulder

The shoulder primal of the sheep carcass is an economical cut, albeit relatively fatty and bony. When cooked slowly, the fatty network breaks down and tenderizes the meat.

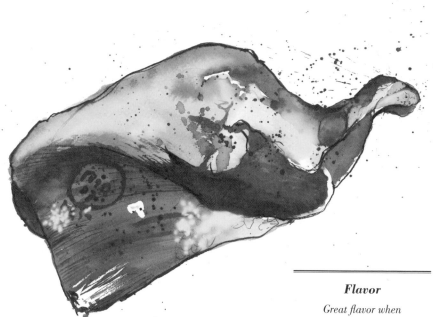

Flavor
Great flavor when cooked slowly.

Cooking
Shoulder cuts are best suited to slow cooking in liquid, such as braising or stewing, to break down the connective tissue.

Neck

Cuts from the neck can be bone-in or boneless fillets.

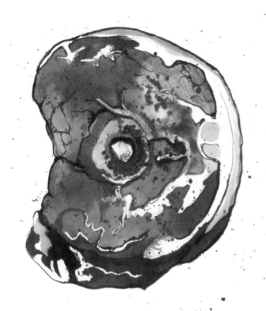

Flavor

The neck is naturally quite tough as it is worked hard by the animal, however it has great flavor when cooked slowly.

Cooking

Cuts from the neck are best slowly cooked in liquid, such as braising or stewing, to break down the connective tissue. Cook them on the bone for extra flavor and texture. Cuts from the neck are traditionally used in the British dish Lancashire hotpot and in Irish stew.

Also known as

Lamb neck fillets, scrag end (British), stewing lamb, middle neck, and lamb neck pieces.

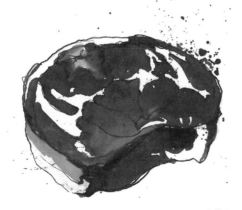

Round- or square-cut shoulder roast and boneless rolled shoulder

This large, round, or square-shaped cut can be bone-in or boneless; if the bones remain in (the shoulder blade, arm bone, and up to seven ribs), it can be sliced into blade chops. The roast is far easier to carve if you ask your butcher to remove the bones first. With the bones removed it is sold as boneless shoulder or boneless rolled shoulder for stews and curries.

Flavor

Good flavor when cooked correctly.

Cooking

Boneless rolled shoulder roast is well suited to marinating and stuffing before roasting. Shoulder responds best to roasting at a slightly lower temperature for a little longer. Blade chops are best suited to braising.

Also known as

Round cut, shoulder roast, lamb round- or square-cut shoulder, and shoulder block.

Blade chops

These are economical chops cut from the shoulder blade.

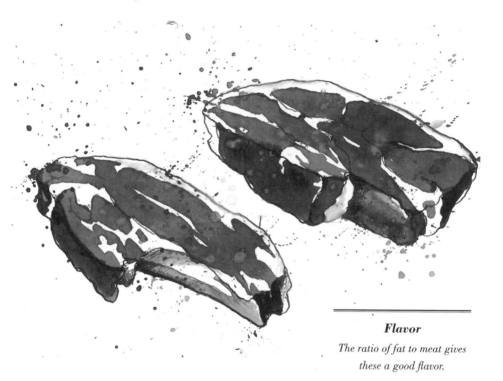

Flavor

The ratio of fat to meat gives these a good flavor.

Cooking

Blade chops are best broiled, roasted, fried, or braised.

Also known as

Shoulder chops, shoulder blade chops, and shoulder blade lamb chops.

Fore shank

This is the fore leg of the sheep, taken from the lower end of the shoulder primal. It is a smaller cut than the hind shank.

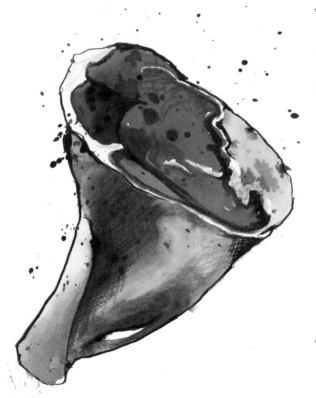

Flavor

Lamb shank is relatively lean, but it becomes tender and flavorful when cooked slowly.

Cooking

It is best suited to long, slow cooking such as braising to break down the connective tissue. The meat from the shank can also be ground or cut into cubes for stews. Lamb shanks can also replace veal shanks in osso buco.

Also known as

Lamb shank, lamb trotter, and shin.

Breast

Lamb breast is cut from the forequarter of the sheep and includes part of the belly. Lamb spareribs are cut from here.

Flavor

Breast is a relatively fatty cut, streaked with fat. It is sweet-tasting and flavorful.

Cooking

It is best suited to stuffing and roasting, braising, barbecuing, or pot-roasting.

Also known as

Poitrine d'agneau *(French).*

Flavor

Spareribs are full of flavor though they can be somewhat fatty.

Cooking

Spareribs are best marinated then broiled, grilled, or braised.

Also known as

Denver-style ribs. If the spareribs are cut into long, skinny individual ribs, they are known as riblets; originally this was an economical way of making them go further.

Spareribs

Lamb breast spareribs are cut from the breast primal and contain the rib bones with the meat and fat in between.

Rack

This is an expensive primal and makes an impressive roast to serve at the table. Rack of lamb consists of eight rib bones, backbone, and the rib-eye muscle. It slices easily into tender chops and cutlets. A crown roast is made by curving and tying two racks together into a circle and sitting them upright on the backbone. A guard of honor is made by criss-crossing two racks together.

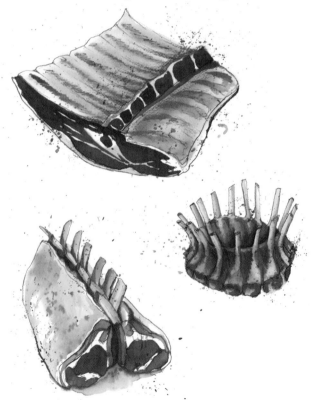

Flavor

Succulent, tender, and sweet, thanks to the rib bones.

Cooking

Rack of lamb is best suited to roasting. Chops and cutlets can be grilled or barbecued.

Also known as

Best end (British), rib roast. Boneless cuts from the best end are known as cannons (British) and carrés d'agneau (French). Cannon of lamb is a boneless fillet taken from the rack.

Rib chops and cutlets

Rib chops are cut from the rib roast. If the fat is trimmed away from the end of the bone they are known as having been Frenched. If the chine bone (backbone) has been removed they are described as chined.

Flavor

They are tender, meaty, and sweet, thanks to the rib-eye muscle and rib bones.

Cooking

Rib chops are best suited to broiling, grilling, frying, roasting, and barbecuing.

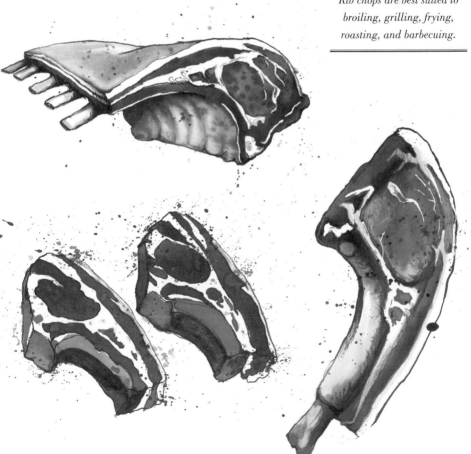

Loin

Cuts from the loin primal are expensive, tender, and flavorful.
The loin primal contains the chine bone, but this can be
removed to create a boneless roast which is ideal for stuffing,
rolling, and tying. It can also be cut into lean, boneless
pieces called noisettes.

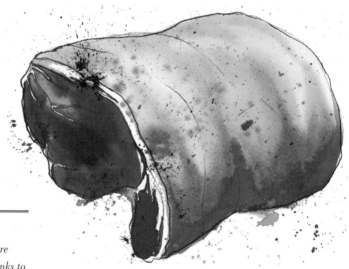

Flavor

Cuts from the loin are
succulent and juicy, thanks to
the extra fat for basting.

Cooking

Larger cuts from the loin
are best suited to roasting.
Noisettes can be fried or
grilled. Lamb loin chops can
be fried, broiled, or barbecued.

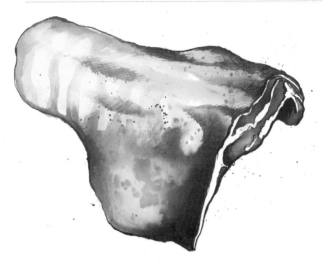

Loin roast and saddle of lamb

The loin roast is cut from the loin primal. A saddle of lamb consists
of the two loin roasts, one from each side of the sheep carcass, joined
together by the backbone. It makes an impressive roast and is ideal for
serving a crowd, although it is an expensive choice.

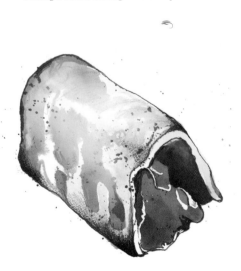

Loin chops and double loin chops

Loin chops are an expensive cut. They contain the eye of the loin and the chine bone (backbone). Double loin chops are cut across the backbone and are generous in size. They consist of the top loin and tenderloin. The bone can be removed and the chops cut and rolled into boneless chops known as noisettes of lamb.

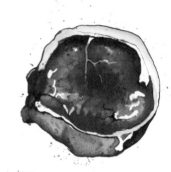

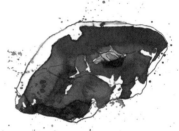

Flavor

Lean and flavorsome.

Cooking

Loin and double loin chops are best suited to broiling, grilling, or frying. Double loin chops can also be roasted.

Also known as

T-bone chops, Barnsley chops (British), center loin chops (Irish).

Strip loin

The strip loin is a boneless strip cut from the loin. It consists of the loin eye muscle and is an expensive cut.

Flavor

This is a lean and tender cut.

Cooking

It is best suited to gentle cooking, such as braising or slow roasting.

Also known as

Boneless loin. The strip loin can also be called cannon, similar to the one cut from the rack.

Tenderloin and medallions

The slim tenderloin can be cut into slices called medallions. One lamb tenderloin will serve just one person. Because it is so small, it is usually left attached to the strip loin.

Flavor

Incredibly tender and flavorsome.

Cooking

Tenderloin is often rolled in herbs and spices before being roasted or fried.

Also known as

Fillet.

Leg

***The leg primal cut is the hind leg of the sheep or carcass.
It is relatively expensive and can be cut in half, if required,
into the larger shank and the smaller top end.***

The leg bone can be removed and the boned meat can then be stuffed, rolled, and tied, or slashed open on both sides to increase the surface area (butterflied) for roasting, broiling, or barbecuing. The leg can be cut into numerous small roasts and can also be cut into cubes for stewing, braising, or kabobs.

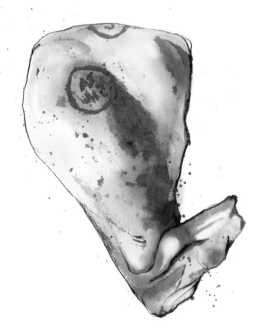

Flavor

*Leg is lean, yet succulent
and flavorsome when
cooked correctly.*

Cooking

*Cuts from the leg can be
roasted or cooked slowly
in liquid, such as braising,
stewing, or pot-roasting.*

Shank

The shank is the lower part of the leg from the knee to the ankle.
Some shanks can be cut more generously to include part of the loin
from higher up the leg.

Flavor

*Tender and flavorsome
when cooked slowly.*

Cooking

*The lower shank section is best
suited to long, slow cooking
in liquid, such as braising,
stewing, or pot-roasting.*

Also known as

*Knuckle of lamb (British)
and shank of lamb.*

Top end

The top end of leg can be bone-in or boned. It is good value and makes a popular roast for a gathering. If the hip bone has been removed it is easier to carve. A center leg roast is a leg of lamb with the shank taken off at the knee. Center leg slices may be cut from here.

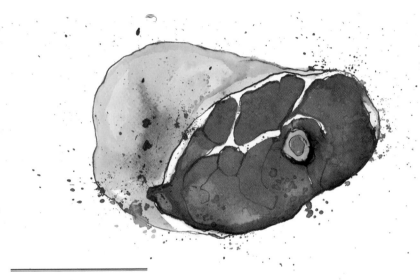

Flavor
Leg of lamb is lean and tender.

Cooking
It is best suited to roasting and is best served pink; it can dry out if overcooked.

Also known as
Center cut lamb leg.

Boneless leg roast

This leg roast is boned, trimmed, rolled, and tied.

Flavor

It has great flavor due to its natural coating of fat, which bastes the tender meat as it cooks. Sometimes the fat is removed, in which case it is a relatively lean cut.

Cooking

Best suited to searing over a high heat, then roasting

Chump roast and chump chops

The chump roast is cut from the top of the leg where it meets the loin and can be bone-in or boneless. Chump chops can be cut from here; further down the leg they become leg steaks. One chump roast will feed two people.

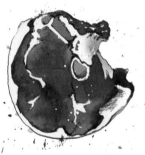

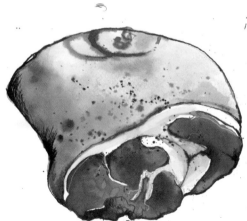

Flavor

Relatively lean but still tender and meaty.

Cooking

Take care not to overcook because it can dry out easily.

Also known as

Foremost section of the leg.

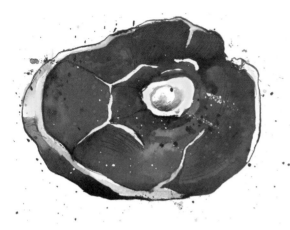

Flavor

Flavorsome when cooked correctly.

Cooking

Chops are best suited to braising, broiling, and grilling. Take care not to overcook because they can dry out easily.

Also known as

Lamb leg chops and lamb leg steaks.

Round leg chops and steaks

These can be cut into bone-in or boneless chops and steaks.

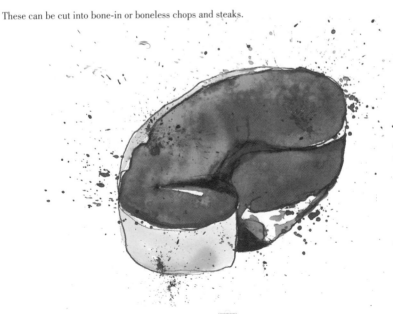

Variety meats

Variety meats are cuts taken from the extremities of the animal or the organs within. They are also known as offal or innards.

Liver

Lambs' liver is less tender and a little stronger in flavor than calves' liver. It is pink and smooth-textured and can be fried in butter with bacon and onions, broiled, or braised. Lambs' liver is one of the ingredients in the traditional Scottish dish haggis. It is also known as lambs' fry.

Kidneys

Lambs' kidneys are single-lobed. Always make sure they are as fresh as possible because they can deteriorate rapidly. Lambs' kidneys are particularly good fried with bacon.

Sweetbreads

Sweetbreads is the culinary name given to the delicately flavored thymus glands (in the throat) and pancreas (in the stomach) of the sheep. Lambs' sweetbreads are usually cheaper than calves' and rarely less tender; those from mutton are tougher, and less edible than lambs'. Sweetbreads are good fried with lambs' brains and liver. See page 237 for advice on preparing them.

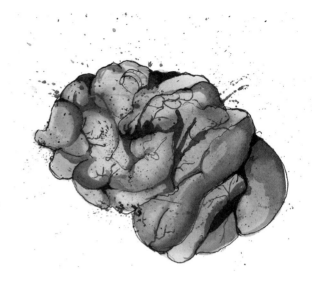

Heart

Fresh lamb's heart should be red and firm. To prepare, rinse in cold water then remove any blood vessels or clots. It is best suited to long, slow cooking in liquid, such as stewing or braising, until it becomes tender. Lamb's heart is one of the key ingredients in the traditional Scottish dish haggis.

Tongue

Lamb's tongue is relatively small. It is best cooked by poaching in stock until tender, before being skinned. It can then be pickled, set into a cold jelly, or fried.

Lungs

Lambs' lungs are bright pink, soft, and spongy and are one of the key ingredients in the traditional Scottish dish haggis. They are also known as lights.

Brains

Lambs' brains should be plump and fresh. To prepare, remove any visible clots, then soak in cold water, changing the water frequently. Poach briefly in water and vinegar, then either eat them cold in a vinaigrette or flour and fry them with herbs until sweet-tasting and creamy textured. Lambs' brains are particularly popular in European and Lebanese dishes.

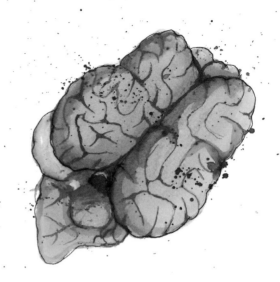

Testicles

Lambs' testicles are small and pale pink in color, with a soft, creamy texture, and a mild, delicate flavor when cooked. Eaten on ranches in the American West and in the Middle East, lambs' testicles are considered a forgotten delicacy by some. They are sold skinned and ready for cooking by frying, and are commonly known as lamb fries.

Meat from sheep of different ages

Suckling lamb

Suckling lamb is lamb that has been slaughtered up to five weeks of age, has only ever been fed on its mother's milk, and has never grazed outdoors. As a consequence, its meat is pale, delicate, and tender. Suckling lamb is usually roasted whole and makes a great feast for a crowd; sometimes suckling lambs are spit-roasted for religious celebrations and festivals. It is also known as milk-fed lamb and baby lamb.

Spring lamb

The main lambing season is in the spring, but spring lamb sold at this time is not lambs born in the spring, because they would be far too young; instead, spring lamb refers to lambs born the previous November and December that are just about old enough for slaughtering in the spring. Spring lamb is often intensively reared for the Easter market by being kept indoors on a controlled diet. It is also known as Easter lamb.

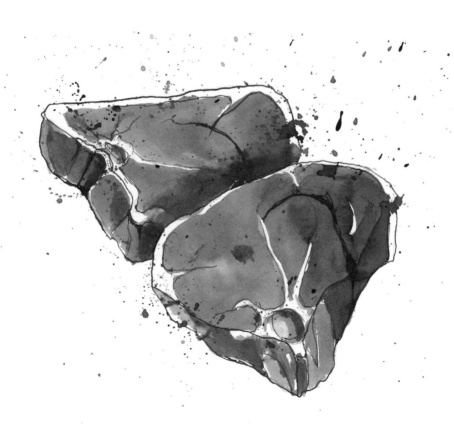

Hogget

A sheep that is slaughtered between one and two years of age is known
as hogget. Meat from a hogget is more strongly flavored than lamb.
Shoulder of hogget can be slow-roasted, braised, or stewed until tender.

Mutton

A sheep that is at least two years old is known as mutton. The carcass requires aging by hanging. Mutton is a darker, more flavorful, and fattier meat than lamb. Cuts from the leg, shoulder, loin, or neck are most commonly used. Mutton becomes tender when slow-roasted or braised or simmered into a broth.

Techniques

Open-boning and butterflying a leg of lamb

To remove the bone, use a long-bladed boning knife and hold it like a dagger, pointing the tip downward as you cut through the meat. Start at the knuckle end and cut through the firmer side of the leg, following the bone closely, until you can work it out of the meat. The bone should lift out (reserve it for making a stock), leaving you with a boneless leg of lamb.

Butterflying is a technique that opens out and flattens a piece of boneless meat, increasing its surface area for absorbing flavors, such as marinades, helping it to cook quickly and evenly, and making it easy to carve. Butterfly joints are usually applied to leg cuts.

Lay the boned leg out on a board. You may wish to remove some of the fat from the outside of the leg, leaving just a thin covering. Then, following the natural grain, make slashes through the meat at regular intervals all over, using a sharp knife. Turn the meat over and repeat on the other side, taking care not to cut all the way through from one slash to another. The idea is to flatten the meat out as evenly as possible. Butterflied leg of lamb can be marinated before being broiled, or barbecued.

Preparing a rack of lamb

To prepare for roasting, lift the skin from one corner
and pull it up and across the fat and meat to remove
it—it should come away in one piece. The chine
bone (backbone) must be removed and discarded, if
your butcher has not already done so. You will need
to do this with a small saw, separating the chine
bone from the rib bones, until it comes away.

Next, use a sharp knife to cut away the piece
of cartilage that sits within the meat and fat at
the thinner end of the rack; remove it with your
fingers. Also remove the rubbery tendon that lies
between the fat and meat. Turn the rack over so it
is fat-side up. Make a horizontal cut across the fat,
approximately 1 inch from the tips of the bones.
Remove the fat to expose the ends of the bones,
then cut between each bone, trimming and scraping
the bones to remove all the fat, to expose the tips
of the bones. Finally, carefully cut away the fat
covering the back of the rack so that only a thin
layer remains.

The rack of lamb may be roasted whole or chopped
into cutlets and grilled or fried until tender and just
pink inside.

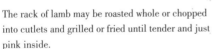

Preparing a guard of honor

A guard of honor is made by interlocking the rib bones of two prepared racks of lamb.

Place each prepared rack of lamb flat-side down on a board so they face each other, with the bones pointing upward. Holding one in each hand, push the racks together, so the bones interlock in a criss-cross fashion.

Using kitchen string, tie down through the guard of honor at regular intervals to hold the racks together.

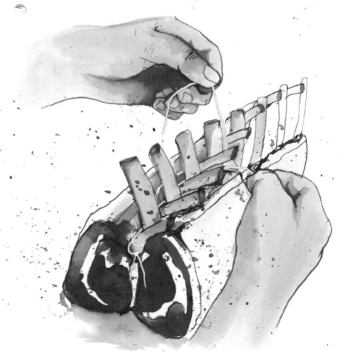

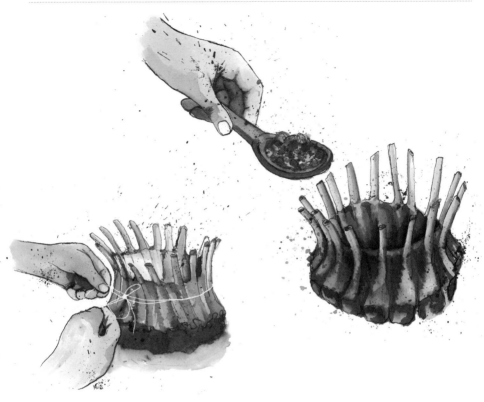

Assembling a crown roast

A crown roast is made from two prepared racks of lamb that are curved and tied together into a circle and roasted.

To assemble a crown roast, hold each rack flat-side down and bend each into a semicircle with the fat on the inside (if the rack is too rigid to bend, make a small cut between each cutlet to give it a little more flexibility). Using a thick needle and thread, sew the racks together vertically down each side to form

a circle. Tie some string around the "waist" of the crown to secure it further.

Before roasting, a crown roast is traditionally stuffed with a vegetarian stuffing, such as a mixture of bread crumbs and herbs.

To serve, slice into cutlets and serve each with a little of the stuffing.

Preparing a saddle of lamb for roasting

Two loins that are still joined together are known as a saddle of lamb. This cut makes a great roast that will easily serve 10 to 12 people.

To prepare, cut away any excess fat from underneath the saddle and around the edges. Remove the kidneys.

Place the saddle on a board, back-fat side up. The hip (aitch) bone should be protruding from one end. Using a small, sharp knife, lift the skin from one corner of the saddle and pull it up and across the fat and meat to remove it—it should come away in one piece. Discard the skin, then score the back fat evenly all over in a criss-cross fashion.

Testing lamb for doneness

Lamb should be cooked until at least
medium-rare—that is, until at least slightly
pink and without any traces of blood—with
a core temperature of 130–140°F (55–60°C).
Insert a meat thermometer into the meat
before roasting—so you can check the
temperature without opening the oven
door—or test when the roast is almost cooked.
To take an accurate reading, the thermometer
should be inserted into the thickest part
of the meat and held for 15 seconds. If the
thermometer is inserted before roasting,
remove the roast just before it reaches 130°F
(55°C), because the meat will carry on
cooking while it rests.

Preparing kidneys

Lambs' kidneys are single-lobed and are relatively straightforward to prepare. First remove the outer membrane and any blood vessels. Cut in half and remove the central fatty core, then rinse in cold water. Lambs' kidneys may be fried or broiled until just pink inside, or cooked slowly in liquid, such as in a braise or stew.

Preparing sweetbreads

Lambs' sweetbreads are not considered such a
delicacy as calves' sweetbreads, but they do make
a tasty dish. Both types of sweetbread—from
the thymus gland and from the stomach—can be
prepared by repeatedly soaking in fresh water, until
they turn white. Blanch the soaked sweetbreads
in boiling, salted water for 1 to 2 minutes, drain,
then refresh under cold water. Press them dry with
a clean dish towel, dust with flour, and fry until
hot and creamy inside. Blanched sweetbreads can
also be roasted, braised, or gently poached in an
aromatic broth for 45 minutes or until tender.

Fried lamb with paprika and vinegar

This garlic-spiked dish using shoulder of lamb is quick to make and full of spicy flavors.

Serves 4

1 slice stale bread
3 tbsp red wine vinegar
3 tbsp olive oil
1¾ lb lean lamb
shoulder, diced
6 garlic cloves, minced
½ dried chile pepper,
seeded and sliced
1 tbsp paprika
½ tsp ground cloves
4 tbsp finely chopped parsley

Sprinkle the bread with the vinegar. Heat 2 tbsp oil in a large skillet or Dutch oven and fry the bread for 3 to 4 minutes until golden. Remove from the pan and set aside.

Add the remaining oil, lamb, half the garlic, and the chile to the pan and fry over a high heat, stirring constantly, for 10 minutes or until the lamb is golden. Add the paprika, cloves, remaining garlic, parsley, and a scant cup (7 fl oz) water. Cover and cook for 30 minutes or until the lamb is tender and the liquid has reduced.

Cut or blend the fried bread into crumbs, then stir into the lamb mixture to thicken the sauce.

Honeyed lamb

This rich Moroccan tagine was originally devised as a way of preserving meat before refrigeration. Make it 24 hours in advance, then reheat when required. If ras el hanout—a North African herb and spice mix—is not available locally, try mail order websites such as www.theepicentre.com or www.thespicehouse.com.

A pinch of saffron threads
1 tsp freshly ground
black pepper
1 tsp ground cinnamon
2 tsp ras el hanout
2 lb middle neck of lamb
with bone in
1 cup (6 oz) raisins
3 onions, finely chopped
1 cup (5 oz) blanched almonds
1¼ cups (14 oz) honey
Juice of ½ lemon

Crush the saffron with the other spices and a pinch of salt using a pestle and mortar. Rub most of the mixture into the lamb and mix the remainder with the raisins.

Put the marinated lamb, onions, almonds, and ⅔ cup (6 fl oz) water into a pan. Bring to a boil then cover and cook gently, stirring occasionally, for about 1 to 1¼ hours until the meat is almost tender—top up with more water if necessary to keep the meat from catching on the bottom of the pan.

Stir in the raisin mixture, honey, and lemon juice and cook, uncovered, for 30 minutes until almost all the liquid has evaporated, leaving a rich, thick sauce. Serve with couscous.

Tray kibbeh

This Lebanese dish using ground lamb, bulghur, and spices makes a delicious main course. It can also be served as an appetizer.

Serves 4–6

½ cup (4 fl oz) tomato juice
¼ cup (2 fl oz) fresh
lemon juice
1 cup (7 oz) bulghur
½ cup (2 oz) whole wheat flour
1 lb ground lamb
1 tsp paprika
½ tsp ground cumin
A large pinch of cayenne
1½ tbsp sesame seeds
¼ cup (2 oz) butter, melted
2 tbsp sunflower oil

For the filling:
1 tbsp olive oil
1 onion, finely chopped
12 oz ground lamb
½ cup (2 oz) walnuts, chopped
½ tsp allspice

First make the kibbeh "pastry." Mix together the tomato juice, lemon juice, bulghur, and ½ cup (4 fl oz) water. Let rest for 10 minutes.

Put 1 lb ground lamb, the spices, and the sesame seeds into a food processor and process until the meat is ground into a paste-like consistency. Gradually add the bulghur mixture, then season with salt and pepper. Tip into a bowl, mix well, and chill for 2 hours.

Meanwhile, make the filling. Heat the olive oil in a skillet and fry the onion for 5 minutes until soft. Add the ground lamb and fry, stirring, for 5 to 10 minutes until the meat is browned. Drain off any excess fat, then stir in the nuts and allspice and season with salt and pepper.

Preheat the oven to 400°F (200°C).

Mix together the butter and sunflower oil and brush over the bottom of a square baking pan. Using wet hands, press half the pastry mixture into the base of the pan. Spoon over the filling, spreading it evenly. Press the remaining pastry over the top, pressing it up to the edges of the pan. Cut into eight slices and brush with the remaining sunflower mixture. Bake for 10 minutes, then lower the heat to 350°F (180°C) and bake for a further 30 minutes.

Let cool slightly, then lift out the slices and serve.

Spiced lamb topped with tomatoes

Cooked slowly under a blanket of well-browned onions, these lamb shanks become wonderfully succulent and tender.

Serves 6

Mix together the cinnamon, cumin, ginger, parsley, and cilantro. Divide the mixture and reserve half. Coat the lamb shanks in half the spice mixture, then chill for 3–4 hours.

Heat 2½ tbsp oil in a large Dutch oven. Add the onion, season with salt, and cook gently, stirring occasionally, for 10 to 15 minutes until golden. Remove from the pan.

Preheat the oven to 325°F (170°C).

Add the marinated lamb to the Dutch oven, adding more oil if necessary, and cook for 10 to 15 minutes until browned all over. Season with salt and pepper, then add the remaining spice mixture and the cooked onions.

Put the tomato paste in a cup and blend in a little water. Add to the lamb with enough water to cover. Bring to a boil, cover with a tight-fitting lid, then bake for 1 hour 40 minutes or until the lamb is cooked.

Add the tomatoes, cut-side down, to the pan, sprinkle with the sugar, and return to the oven for 20 minutes or until everything is tender.

1½ tsp ground cinnamon
¼ tsp ground cumin
¼ tsp ground ginger
1 small bunch
parsley, chopped
1 small bunch
cilantro, chopped
6 lamb shanks, each weighing
about ½ lb
3 tbsp olive oil
1 large red onion, finely
chopped
1½ tbsp tomato paste
3 large, ripe tomatoes, peeled,
seeded, and halved
1–2 tsp white sugar

Sautéed lamb with eggplant

This quick, no-fuss recipe is a simple way to add fresh flavors to lamb cutlets.

Serves 4

Heat 1 tbsp olive oil in a wok over a high heat until almost smoking. Add the lamb cutlets and fry for 5 minutes on each side until golden. Remove from the wok and keep warm.

Add the remaining oil to the wok and fry the eggplant with the garlic for 10 to 15 minutes until lightly browned on both sides. Add the tomato slices and stir-fry for 1 minute. Season with salt and pepper, then transfer to a serving dish. Top with the cutlets and garnish with lemon slices and mint.

To make the sauce, mix together the mint and yogurt, season with black pepper, and serve with the lamb and vegetables.

3 tbsp olive oil
8 lamb cutlets, trimmed
2 large eggplants,
thickly sliced
2 garlic cloves, minced
6 large tomatoes, blanched,
skinned, and thickly sliced
1 lemon, sliced, to garnish

For the sauce:
2 tbsp fresh mint, chopped,
plus extra to garnish
²⁄₃ cup (5 fl oz) plain yogurt

Rack of lamb in a garlic crust

This is an easy recipe that makes an impressive roast to serve at the table.

Serves 4–6

Turn the lamb racks bone-side up and cut a narrow slit between each cutlet at the meaty end. Slice 1 garlic clove and stuff each slit with a sliver of the garlic and a blade of rosemary.

Put the lamb racks, fat-side up, into an oiled roasting pan. Cut several shallow slashes into the fat.

Mince the remaining garlic cloves and mix with the bread crumbs, jelly, parsley, and mustard. Season with salt and pepper, then smear over the lamb racks. Let marinate for 1 to 2 hours.

Preheat the oven to 450°F (230°C) and roast the lamb for 25 to 35 minutes until browned and still a little pink in the center.

2 racks of lamb, each
containing 4–6 cutlets, chined
3 garlic cloves
1 rosemary sprig
1 tbsp oil
3 tbsp fresh white
bread crumbs
2 tbsp redcurrant
jelly, warmed
1 tbsp chopped parsley
½ tsp French mustard

Spicy lamb stew with mint and sage

Delicately tender lamb tenderloin is the perfect cut in this traditional Greek pilaf. Use twice the quantity of fresh mint and sage if you prefer.

Serves 6–8

¼ cup (2 fl oz) olive oil
2 lb lean lamb tenderloin, cut into 1-inch cubes
1 onion, chopped
2 carrots, diced
½ cup (4 fl oz) dry white wine
⅔ cup (2½ oz) slivered almonds
1⅓ cups (9 oz) long-grain rice
⅓ cup (2 oz) golden raisins
½ tsp dried sage
1 tsp dried mint

Heat the oil in a large saucepan. Add the lamb and cook, turning regularly, until evenly browned. Add the onion and carrots and cook for 5 minutes. Stir in the wine and season with salt and pepper. Bring to a boil, cover, and cook for 10 minutes.

Meanwhile, toast the almonds in a heavy skillet until lightly golden. Set aside.

Stir 3¾ cups (30 fl oz) water into the meat mixture and simmer for 30 minutes, stirring occasionally. Add the rice, golden raisins, sage, and mint to the stew, then simmer, covered, for 30 to 35 minutes, adding a little extra water if necessary, until the rice is cooked and the meat is tender.

Lamb with apricot sauce

This delicious recipe is inspired by the classic Middle Eastern combination of lamb with apricots, a fusion given added sweetness here with the peanut butter-based sauce.

Serves 4

Cut the lamb into 1-inch cubes and season. Thread onto skewers and broil, or cook in hot oil or melted butter in a skillet until tender, approximately 5 minutes.

To prepare the sauce, melt the oil and butter together and add the garlic. Whisk in the puréed apricots and the peanut butter. Do not allow the peanut butter to become too hot; remove from the pan when half-melted. Add the lemon juice and season to taste. Serve with the lamb pieces. Garnish with parsley.

1½ lb lamb fillet
Salt and freshly ground black
pepper
Oil or butter, to fry
For the sauce:
¼ cup vegetable oil
½ stick butter
1 tsp garlic, minced
6 oz pitted apricots, puréed
⅓ cup peanut butter
Juice of 1 lemon, to taste
Salt and freshly ground black
pepper
Parsley, to garnish

Lamb chops with cheese

An unusual but delicious combination of lamb and cheese, cooked in foil packages to retain all of the natural flavors.

Serves 4

2 tbsp butter
1 onion, sliced
2 garlic cloves, minced
4 lamb chump chops
3 tomatoes, sliced
3 tsp dried oregano
4 oz Gruyère cheese,
thinly sliced

Preheat the oven to 350°F (180°C). Lay a large sheet of aluminum foil on a work surface.

Melt the butter in the skillet and fry the onion and garlic for 3 minutes. Divide the onion mixture between the lamb chops together with the tomatoes, oregano, and cheese. Season with salt and pepper.

Gather up the sides of the foil and pinch together to encase the chops. Transfer to a baking sheet and cook for 1½ to 2 hours until the meat is tender.

Grilled butterflied leg of lamb

An easy, yet delicious, way to add stacks of flavor to a leg of lamb. Boning and butterflying the leg first will ensure it cooks quickly and evenly.

Serves 8–10

Put the lamb into a large dish. Put the garlic, chopped rosemary, sea salt, olive oil, lemon juice, and black pepper in a bowl. Mix well, then rub into the lamb. Marinate for 4 hours or overnight in the refrigerator.

Preheat the barbecue, broiler, or grill to high. Grill the lamb, covered (if your barbecue has a lid), for 30 to 40 minutes, turning regularly. Cook until just pink inside, then garnish with extra rosemary sprigs.

*6 lb leg of lamb, boned and
butterflied (ask your butcher to
do this or see page 230)
8 garlic cloves, thinly sliced
4 tbsp chopped rosemary,
plus 3 sprigs
1 tbsp sea salt
¼ cup (2 fl oz) olive oil
Juice of 2 lemons
2 tsp ground black pepper*

Tung-Po mutton

This dish is a great way of adding lots of flavor to mutton—the slow cooking time allows the meat to become meltingly tender.

Serves 4

Oil, for frying
1 lb stewing mutton, cut into
¾-inch cubes
2 potatoes, cut into
¾-inch cubes
2 carrots, cut into
¾-inch cubes
2 tbsp soy sauce
1 tbsp sugar
2 scallions
1 slice gingerroot
1 garlic clove, crushed
1 tsp five-spice powder
3 tbsp rice wine or dry sherry
½ tsp Szechuan pepper

Heat the oil in a large skillet or wok until almost smoking. Add the mutton and fry for 5 to 6 minutes until golden. Remove from the pan with a slotted spoon, then add the potatoes and carrots. Fry for 5 to 6 minutes until golden.

Put the mutton into a Dutch oven and cover with cold water. Add the remaining ingredients, except for the potato and carrot, then bring to a boil. Reduce the heat and simmer for 2 to 3 hours. Add the potato and carrot, cook for 5 minutes, then serve.

Lisbon liver

Thinly sliced liver that is marinated then cooked with prosciutto is traditionally associated with Lisbon, but is popular throughout Portugal.

Serves 4

Put the liver into a dish with the garlic, bay leaf, wine, and vinegar. Season, then cover and chill for at least 4 hours or preferably overnight.

Remove the liver from the wine mixture—reserving the liquid—and pat dry with paper towels. Discard the bay leaf.

Heat the olive oil in a large pan. Add the prosciutto and cook until crisp. Add the marinated liver and cook for 3 minutes on each side. Transfer the meat to a warm plate, cover, and keep warm.

Stir the reserved wine mixture into the pan and boil rapidly until reduced by about half. Pour over the liver and prosciutto and serve.

1 lb lamb's liver, thinly sliced
4 garlic cloves, minced
1 bay leaf
¾ cup (6 fl oz) dry white wine
1 tbsp white wine vinegar
3 tbsp olive oil
2 oz prosciutto or
bacon, chopped

CREDITS

The author would like to thank the following people and organizations for the information and advice they provided:

Trevor Amen, National Cattlemen's Beef Association (www.beefitswhatsfordinner.com)
American Lamb Board (www.americanlamb.com)
Nigel Armstrong (www.meatcity.ltd.uk)
National Pork Board (www.theotherwhitemeat.com)

BIBLIOGRAPHY

Chartered Institute of Environmental Health, *Food Safety First Principles* (Chadwick House Group, 2005)
Hugh Fearnley-Whittingstall, *The River Cottage Meat Book* (Hodder & Stoughton, 2004)
Aliza Green, *Field Guide to Meat* (Quirk Books, 2005)
Larousse Gastronomique (Hamlyn, 2001)
Harold McGee, *McGee on Food & Cooking* (Hodder & Stoughton, 2004)
John J. Mettler Jr, *Basic Butchering of Livestock and Game* (Storey Publishing, 2003)
Susan Spaull and Lucinda Bruce-Gardyne, *Leiths Techniques Bible* (Bloomsbury, 2003)
OXO Ltd, *The Book of Meat Cookery*
Charles Sinclair, *Dictionary of Food* (A & C Black, 2005)
Michael Van Straten, *Super Feast* (Little Books Ltd, 2005)